Horizons & Hopes

The Future of Religious Education

Edited by

THOMAS H. GROOME

and

HAROLD DALY HORELL

Paulist Press
New York/Mahwah, N.J.

Library of Congress Cataloging-in-Publication Data

    Horizons & hopes : the future of religious education / edited by Thomas H. Groome and Harold Daly Horell.
       p. cm.
    Includes bibliographical references.
    ISBN 0-8091-4154-X
    1. Christian education. I. Title: Horizons and hopes. II. Groome, Thomas H. III. Horell, Harold Daly.

BV1471.3 .H67 2003
268'.82—dc21

                             2002154588

Published by Paulist Press
997 Macarthur Boulevard
Mahwah, New Jersey 07430

www.paulistpress.com

Printed and bound in the United States of America

Contents

105450

Foreword

Edith Prendergast

The poet David Whyte writes that "people are hungry and one good word is bread for a thousand." Many a good word was spoken at Envisioning the Future of Religious Education, a stimulating symposium held at Boston College in June 2000. Captured now in this book, these kernels of wisdom lend renewed vigor and fresh vision to the crucial ministry of religious education.

Much has been written about religious education in the post-conciliar period. What is new in this work is the emphasis given to adult and young-adult faith formation in the context of total catechesis. Influenced by the shift toward postmodernity as well as by the recognition of the importance of making explicit connections between catechesis and spirituality, this collection of essays will be most helpful to all involved in sharing the word of life. In particular, it offers much hope and direction for those who struggle and search for ways to minister appropriately to the post–Vatican II generations.

The poet Gerard Manley Hopkins reminds us of God's pervasive presence and activity in the community. He writes:

> Christ plays in ten thousand places,
> lovely in limbs and lovely in eyes not his,
> to the Father through the features of men's faces.

Foreword

Drawing upon foundational principles from the *General Directory for Catechesis*, Thomas Groome maps out a comprehensive, community-centered paradigm. His paradigm engages parish, family, and school in a collaborative and intentional conversation in order to form, inform, and transform persons and communities into apprentices of Jesus who are sent forth into the world to live their faith in the marketplace. I am heartened by the author's affirmation that the central task of catechetical education is to bring a catechetical consciousness to every aspect of life and ministry and to enable learners to discover God in faces, places, and indeed, in all of life.

Jane Regan's invitation to remold catechesis and to view it through the lens of evangelization strengthens our understanding of evangelizing catechesis. Drawing upon insights from systems thinking and learning organizations of the corporate world, her concept of "learning communities" connects with many of Groome's insights concerning total catechesis. Insisting that the focus must be on adult formation, Regan maintains that faith formation takes place in contexts far beyond any formal catechetical program.

The poet William Blake reminds us:

Unless the eye catch fire, God will not be seen,
Unless the ear catch fire, God will not be heard,
Unless the tongue catch fire, God will not be spoken,
Unless the heart catch fire, God will not be loved.

Grounding catechesis in spirituality, Colleen Griffith addresses the need to foster the relationship between spirituality and religious education. She recognizes the unfortunate split between spirituality and religion and seeks to bring the two into partnership, proposing that the link between them can be effectively explored in catechesis. Furthermore, she highlights the importance of the spirituality of religious educators and suggests that they must allow the heart to "catch fire" in the Spirit.

For Tom Beaudoin, faith formation must respond to the needs of the "generations." He places particular emphasis on the formation of post–Vatican II generations and suggests that their formation takes place as much in the secular culture as in explicitly religious arenas. This he refers to as "virtual" catechesis. But he is careful not to set virtual catechesis in opposition to intentional or "real" catechesis, suggesting, rather, that the interaction of real and virtual catechesis influences the religious identity of the believer and may lead to a new experience of the gospel. His challenge to authenticate the experiences of young adults and to connect these to the faith story gives helpful direction to those involved in ministry with these generations.

Picking up on the generational differences set forth by Beaudoin, Harold Horell brings yet another insight to the fore. He maintains that "Gen X-ers" and the "Millennials" have unique life experiences and, consequently, new perspectives on Christian faith. These two generations draw attention to the gradual yet growing cultural shift affecting all ages. This shift is a movement away from modernity's preoccupation with certitude to postmodernity's embrace of plurality and ambiguity.

Horell notes the tension arising among the postmodern generations. Those embracing postmodernity desire to find new, more authentic ways of connecting with God, self, and others, while those who trivialize postmodernity tend to move beyond or to the fringe of the church. The church becomes for them one of those large institutions to which they respond with suspicion or even contempt. The challenge for religious educators in the midst of this cultural shift is to affirm the positive, questing dimensions of postmodernity, enter into genuine conversation about meaning and value, and remain open to discernment of God's ongoing call in everyday experience.

Having discussed the challenges and hopes at the core of the ministry of religious education, Maryanne Confoy quite eloquently addresses the heart of the matter: God's initiative in our lives. Becoming aware that God is madly in love with us calls us to respond in love to God, while at the same time deepening our relationships with one another. Neither catechesis nor evangelization is possible or effective without the action of God working through the power of the Spirit. God is, in fact, the one who inspires and sustains all catechetical work and all who do this work.

This volume will be a very useful resource for catechetical leaders as they explore fresh and comprehensive initiatives in the ministry of religious education. The wisdom shared in these pages is a source of encouragement and offers valuable insights to all who serve in catechetical ministry. The attention given to adult and young-adult formation is very helpful at a time when many tend to view the church with cynicism and skepticism. Its holistic approach, as well as its focus on God's gracious initiative, engenders a trust that sustains and a hope that endures.

—Edith Prendergast, R.S.C.
Director, Office of Religious Education
Archdiocese of Los Angeles

1

=====

Total Catechesis/
Religious Education:
A Vision for Now and Always

Thomas H. Groome

I put catechesis and religious education together in my title, not because I can't decide between them but to pose the two as symbiotic, as dual and necessary emphases within "education in faith." Catholics tend to use *catechesis* to describe the *formative* process of nurturing Christian identity, and *religious education* as *informative* pedagogy in a faith tradition. But, once and for all, let us reject religious education that pretends to teach objectively about religion, that is, religious education that does not engage and affect people's lives. Likewise, let us beware of catechesis that unreflectively socializes people into church membership without education in the spiritual wisdom of Christian Faith.

Both religious education and catechesis are necessary for educating the Christian person and community. With an appropriate pedagogy—as I summarize later—both can be done as dual emphases within the same enterprise. (To signal my commitment to the values of each and to avoid awkward repetition, I will favor the phrase *catechetical education* throughout this essay.)

The word *total* in my title intimates my overall proposal of a comprehensive and community-centered paradigm that forges *a coalition of*

1

parish, family, and school or parish program, engaging all aspects of these communities and their every member in sharing faith together for lifelong conversion as disciples of Jesus for the reign of God. I will unpack this proposal in conversation with the *General Directory for Catechesis.*

On August 15, 1997, the Congregation for the Clergy—the Vatican agency entrusted with oversight of catechetical education—issued a new *General Directory for Catechesis* (hereafter GDC). The GDC replaces even as it builds upon the *General Catechetical Directory* of 1971. Like its predecessor, it is likely to set the tone and tenor of catechetical education for the coming era in the Catholic Church. It provides a focus for the reflection throughout this essay. Though the document is distinctly Catholic, I hope Protestant readers can "listen in" as "neighbors" in the body of Christ and hear resonant notes for their own ecclesial contexts.

The opening sections of the GDC amount to a description of the nature and purpose of catechetical education. It claims that confusion about purposes is a major cause of "defects and errors" in faith education, that good pastoral practice is possible "only if the nature and end of catechesis…are correctly understood" (no. 9). I agree. So, to explain my overall proposal—*total catechetical education*—I begin with a summary of nature and purpose.

The What and Why of Total Catechetical Education

A "New" Evangelization as Umbrella?

The GDC describes the nature and purpose of catechetical education under the umbrella of evangelization. In summary, the GDC understands evangelization as "the process by which the Church, moved by the Holy Spirit, proclaims and spreads the Gospel throughout the entire world" (no. 48). Then it positions catechesis within evangelization as the more in-depth function of informing and forming Christian identity: "Catechesis, distinct from the primary procla-

2

mation of the Gospel, promotes and matures initial conversion, educates the convert in the faith, and incorporates him into the Christian community" (no. 61). In sum, catechesis is to be "a school of faith, an initiation and apprenticeship in the entire Christian life,...an essential moment in the process of evangelization" (nos. 30, 63).

Though I'm no patristic scholar, my impression is that the first Christian communities recognized *evangelization* and *catechesis* as symbiotic functions—a partnership. The job of the *evangelistes* was to preach the bare-bones kerygma to people who had not heard it already, to arouse interest and to invite to initial Christian faith. Thereafter, the *didaskaloi* (teachers) moved in, as it were, to catechize the newcomers in the *didache* (teaching) and to nurture their Christian identity. The two functions were sequential and complementary rather than hierarchically related, as the GDC might suggest.

Renewed emphasis on evangelization among Catholics is one of the more notable developments of the latter part of the twentieth century. As Avery Dulles notes, for the majority of Catholics "the very term has a Protestant ring."[1] In fact, the work of Karl Barth toward the middle of the twentieth century was a major influence in reviving the term into Christian consciousness. So, it was never mentioned at Vatican I (1869–70), whereas Vatican II (1962–65) mentioned the word *gospel* (*evangelium*) 157 times, *evangelize* 18 times, and *evangelization* 31 times.[2]

After the council, Pope Paul VI continued to recenter evangelization as the baptismal responsibility of all Christians—not just what missionaries do in far off lands. In his 1975 apostolic exhortation *Evangelii Nuntiandi* (hereafter EN), we read: "Evangelization is in fact the grace and vocation proper to the Church, her deepest identity. She exists in order to evangelize" (EN, no. 14).

Under Pope John Paul II the term has continued to expand and gain currency; he has popularized a "new evangelization" to signal a developed understanding. Now the GDC designates evangelization as the umbrella description of the church's whole mission in the world and situates catechesis as one function within it. I'm convinced, however, that this move will be pastorally wise only if we appreciate how much the church has grown in its understanding of evangelization—far beyond its stereotypical meaning for Catholics. This caution is especially urgent in pluralist societies and non-missionary ecclesial contexts. In gist, *the new evangelization is about Catholics renewing enthusiasm for their faith, intensifying their efforts to live it boldly in the world.* Beyond this, I can name five significant developments.

1. Evangelization is about promoting personal encounter and relationship with Jesus Christ. This emphasis has been one of the richest aspects of the new evangelization, a reminder that the "heart" of Christian faith is not scriptures or traditions, not dogmas or doctrines, not churches or sacraments, not creeds or codes—integral as all of these are—but the person of Jesus. Evangelization and catechesis, then, should bring people into "communion and intimacy with Jesus Christ" (no. 80).

I love that the GDC uses "apprenticeship" interchangeably with "discipleship"; apparently the New Testament term *mathetes* can be translated either way. Christian faith will always be personal "following of Jesus" (no. 41) as apprentices to the Master. This is not an individualized affair, however, a "me and Jesus" arrangement. Christian faith is radically communal and yet should be a deeply personal relationship with Jesus Christ—an intimacy of the heart and soul.

2. Evangelization is not so much about "bringing them in" as "bringing us out." For so long Catholics thought of evangelization exclusively as gathering converts into the Catholic Church. Though this could be done anywhere, it was eminently the work of missionaries who went to cultures that had not yet heard the gospel. Even Vatican II understood evangelization as the "mission *ad gentes*"—bringing people into the church who do not yet belong.[3]

By contrast, the church now emphasizes evangelization as bringing Christians out into the world to live their faith in the marketplaces of life. Its focus is not to make non-Catholics into Catholics, but to make Catholics into Christians who live their faith in every arena and on every level—personal, interpersonal, and social/political. This

4

means "bringing the Good News into all the strata of humanity...transforming humanity from within and making it new," participating in God's work of "liberating salvation."⁴ Thus, Christian evangelization is not a narrow spiritual exercise but "the integral development of the whole person and of all peoples" (no. 18). Evangelization "includes a message of liberation" (no. 103), requiring teachers to "arouse in catechumens and those receiving catechesis 'a preferential option for the poor'" (no. 104), to "stir Christian hearts to the cause of justice" (no. 17).

3. *Evangelization is not only toward "peoples where Christ and the Gospel are not known" but should mature the faith of those already Christian and, where necessary, revivify the faith of old Christian cultures* (no. 58). The GDC recognizes that evangelization should always have an accent on missionary activity. Yet, the new evangelization emphasizes both maturing and renewing Christian faith. In other words, all Christians and all communities are always in need of evangelization; none of us has "arrived" in the journey of Christian faith. Particularly urgent is to re-evangelize tired old cultural faith, bringing it to life again in order to permeate its cultural setting (see no. 58). In this "faith alive" effort, the whole church and all members both evangelize and are evangelized.

4. *Evangelization is not only a ministry of the word but engages all of the church's ministries, the realization of its whole mission* (see nos. 46 to 48). Etymologically, evangelization implies a ministry of the word. In Catholic tradition, however, preaching the gospel always meant more than *preaching* the gospel. It also includes celebrating the sacraments; doing the works of justice, peace, and compassion; and building up Christian community. In sum, evangelization is every way that the church continues the mission and ministry of Jesus in the world.

5. *Evangelization must avoid Christian hubris, proceeding with ecumenical sensitivity and openness to dialogue with other religious traditions.* A great gift of Vatican II was its call to Christians to enter into real dialogue with people of other religious traditions. The council urged "truly human conversation" with all peoples of good will, "to learn by sincere and

patient dialogue what treasures a bountiful God has distributed among the nations of the earth."[5] And though the church "must ever proclaim Christ, as 'the way, the truth, and the life,'"[6] their very faith in Jesus should lead Christians into "dialogue and cooperation with the followers of other religions."[7]

So, even as Christians must commit to sharing and bearing witness to their own faith, they must also respect the Spirit's movements throughout humankind and appreciate the many ways that God brings people home to Godself. This caution is made more urgent by regrettable Roman statements that non-Catholics "are in a gravely deficient situation" by way of salvation. Further, clarion calls to Catholics to evangelize can be downright dangerous in the flash points of religious tension (from Belfast to Benares, Sarajevo to the Sudan).

Now, with such developments beyond the old Catholic stereotype of evangelization—as conversion—the term may indeed be a fine umbrella for catechetical education. It may lend us the "fire in the belly" to do it better than ever. However, given the "effective history" (Gadamer) that the term *evangelization* has had, the effort to redefine it remains an uphill struggle. Old Catholics will long think of it exclusively as the mission *ad gentes*.

And while evangelization may be motivating in mission contexts, it seems less likely to enhance catechesis among families and communities already well established in Christian faith. I would never think of my spouse and I as evangelizing our little son, Ted, but certainly we will share our faith with him and, with God's help, inform and form him in Christian identity. Where Christian faith is already well established, spirituality and growth in faith may have more emotive appeal than evangelization as the intent of catechetical education.

A Holistic Affair

Reflecting the developments within a "new evangelization," and thinking especially of an established church, I propose that the nature and purpose of catechetical education is *to inform, form, and transform Christian persons and communities as apprentices to Jesus for God's reign in the world.*

To inform: People are hungrier than ever for a coherent faith that nurtures their spirituality. Catechetical education must provide as much. In terms of content, it should educate people in the spiritual wisdom of Christian faith, thoroughly grounding them in the whole Christian story—its scriptures and traditions, creeds, code of ethics, and ways of worship. In terms of process, it should engage people as active learners, encouraging them to think for themselves, to understand their faith, to make it their own, and to choose to live it.

Instead of a narrow cognitivism, *informing* in Christian faith must reach into the deep heart's core of people's very being—into their souls—educating their heads, hearts, and hands. Instead of unreflective indoctrination, catechetical education should engage people's reason, memory, and imagination to probe and question, to "see for themselves" what the Christian story means for and invites from their lives. Such religious education reaches beyond socialization to lend Christians the understanding and conviction they need to live as disciples of Jesus in the postmodern world. Without such *informing*, the dangers range from fundamentalism to dismissing Christianity as nonsense.

To form: Faith should not be one among many aspects of identity for Christians but the defining sentiment that permeates all else. Christian faith should be a whole way of life reflected in everything that Christians do. This requires catechetical education to be powerfully formative, nurturing people in Christian outlook and commitment, disposing them to live as disciples of Jesus. The formative role of catechesis is a repeated theme throughout the GDC; it calls for "integral formation" (no. 29) in "the entire Christian life" (no. 30).

As I elaborate below, the formative function of catechetical education makes imperative that it engage the family and parish. For how else is identity formed but through the socialization of community? To try to form Christian identity apart from community denies the communal nature of Christian faith and belies the findings of the social sciences, which agree that we are formed, in large part, by our sociocultural contexts. As raising a Polish person requires Polish socialization, and an Irish person Irish socialization, so becoming Christian requires Christian socialization.

To transform: I use this term to capture the lifelong nature of Christian conversion, that it is a journey more than an achievement, a dynamic process rather than a static state. Christian conversion calls us *personally* to lifelong growth in living the way of Jesus, and *socially* to help transform church and society toward God's reign. If we cease to grow in faith, we can readily lose it entirely. If we settle for the church as anything less than "the universal sacrament of salvation for the life of the world" (no. 83), we fail in the social responsibilities of Christian faith. Clearly, Christian conversion takes a lifetime.

Christian faith is to be ever vibrant and vital, life-giving for self and others, for church and society. Pope John Paul II often states the intent of the new evangelization as "faith alive." This is true whether our initiation is gradual through Christian nurture or by an intense experience—falling off the horse on the way to Damascus. Paul still had his "race to run" (2 Tim 4:7) after his conversion and still had to struggle with a "thorn in the flesh" (2 Cor 12:7). As the GDC repeatedly insists, catechetical education must help sustain "the process of continuing conversion" (no. 69), "which lasts for the whole of life" (no. 56). This is why it champions "continuous education in the faith" or "permanent catechesis" (no. 51).

Persons and communities: Christian faith is deeply personal *and* radically communal. Both aspects are integral to it and must be held in fruitful tension to avoid individualism and communalism.

Emphasizing the *personal*, there is no such thing, really, as an anonymous Christian—one without a name. In the lovely imagery of Isaiah, God knows and calls each person by name (see Isa 45:4). Each Christian has his or her personal vocation to holiness as a disciple of Jesus.

Baptism grants every Christian rights and responsibilities that can never be erased or delegated. Within God's family, and explicitly for Christians within the body of Christ, each member is irreplaceable and must function as a full participant—an agent in faith more than a dependent. As Paul explained to the Corinthians, just as "the eye cannot say to the hand, 'I have no need of you,' nor again the head to the feet" (1 Cor 12:21), likewise, each member in the body of Christ has a unique role to play.

Then, emphasizing the *communal*, a private Christian is a contradiction in terms. Christian faith must be lived in and through a community of disciples in the midst of and "for the life of the world" (John 6:51). Since the call of Abraham and Sarah, it has been clear in the Jewish-Christian traditions that our relationship with God is through a people of God. In other words, God comes to us and we go to God as a community—together.

The ecclesial nature of faith has been a particular emphasis in Catholic Christianity. To cite *The Catechism of the Catholic Church*, the church is "the sacrament of salvation, the sign and the instrument of the communion of God and man"[8] Here again, Paul's metaphor of the body of Christ and its unity within diversity is illuminating. "As a body is one though it has many parts, and all the parts of the body, though many, are one body, so also Christ. For in one Spirit we were all baptized into one body, whether Jews or Greeks, slaves or free, and we were all given to drink of one Spirit" (1 Cor 12:12–13). And though the body is made up of "many parts," it is so bonded that "if one part suffers, all the parts suffer with it; if one part is honored, all the parts share its joy" (1 Cor 12:26).

As apprentices to Jesus: Being an apprentice to Jesus means many things, but surely at core it is to follow the way of the Master. However else we schematize Christian faith, it must be realized—incarnated—in a way of life after the example of Jesus. And Christians believe that Jesus not only modeled the way, but as our Lord and Savior—the Christ of faith—is the catalyst of God's grace to so live.

9

We should highlight that being a disciple of Jesus is a very holistic affair. Apprenticeship to Jesus demands a *whole* faith, one that permeates every aspect of human "being," that engages every feature and capacity of people. Jesus' own preaching of the Great Commandment reflects such a comprehensive discipleship. He brought together from his Hebrew tradition the commandments to love God with all one's being (Deut 6:5) and to love the neighbor as oneself (Lev 19:18). He made explicit that these three loves are "like" each other (see Matt 22:39). Christians are to love God, self, and others—the primary law of their faith—with their whole mind, heart, and strength, with all their soul.

Throughout history, this wholeness of Christian faith was reflected in the church's insistence that discipleship entails right belief *(orthodoxia)*, right ethic *(orthopraxia)*, and right worship *(ortholeitourgia)*. The old *Baltimore Catechism* captured well the wholeness of Christian faith with the question "Why did God make you?" The response was "to know...to love...and to serve"—head, heart, and hands. Likewise, the GDC speaks of "the profound unity of the Christian life," which entails, in traditional terms, *lex credendi, lex vivendi,* and *lex orandi*—the "law of belief, of living, and of prayer" (no. 122). Though we may count three aspects to Christian faith, they make up one mosaic, a holistic affair.

For God's reign in the world: There is a great eschatology to Christian faith, a sense of ultimate purpose, of the great difference it should make for here and hereafter. This is variously described as salvation, redemption, liberation, and so on. However, the biblical symbol that best captures the horizon of Christian faith and thus of catechetical education is the reign of God.

Catechists over the centuries have recognized that their work had great ultimate purpose, and often referred to it as the *kingdom of heaven*—the phrase preferred in Matthew's gospel. However, this prompted a sense of purpose pertaining only to the next life, as in saving souls for heaven. Surely catechesis will always have such eternal purpose. But beyond an otherworldly place for souls, scripture scholarship makes clear that God's reign is to begin now for all humankind and every aspect of creation. The intra- and extra-historical nature of God's reign is reflected in how Jesus taught us to pray: first, "thy kingdom come," and then "thy will be done *on earth* as it is *in heaven*." God is to reign now, with people fulfilling God's loving will on this earth with the hope of eternal life.

The Hebrew scriptures portray God's desires for humankind as love and compassion, peace and justice, mercy and forgiveness, freedom *from* all forms of oppression or exclusion, and freedom *for* living in "right relationship" with God, self, others, and creation. The summary word for God's loving will for people and creation is the beautiful term *shalom*. The shalom of God's reign is to be realized on every level of human existence—personal, interpersonal, and political—and throughout creation. And the Bible makes clear that God takes humankind into covenant on behalf of God's reign; we are invited into partnership to actualize God's shalom in the world.

It is fitting that the GDC refers to Jesus with the title of "catechist of the Kingdom of God" (no. 163). It notes that he "proclaimed the Kingdom of God as the urgent and definitive intervention of God in history, and defined this proclamation '*the Gospel*,' that is the Good News" (no. 34). It is good news precisely because God's reign demands "the integral development of the human person and of all people" (no. 18).

Scripture scholars now agree that Jesus understood God's reign as the central purpose of his life and ministry. He subsumed the values it represented in his Hebrew tradition but emphasized and deepened *the law of love* as the "greatest commandment" (Matt 22:36) of God's rule. As noted, he united the three loves—of God, neighbor, and self—as one love with three expressions, and he pushed neighbor to the ultimate inclusion—of enemies. Postmodernity tends to reject universal narratives—overarching frameworks that attempt to give

11

meaning to everything. Yet the reign of God will always be the vision that arises out of our Christian story—particular though it may be.

We capture how comprehensive is God's reign by thinking of it as both/and rather than either/or. So, it is a *spiritual* symbol calling Christians to *holiness* of life and a *social* symbol demanding that they work for *justice* in the world. It should be the disposition of people's own *hearts*, and they must live its values in the *public* arena. It lends hope for life *hereafter* depending on how we live *here*. Commitment to the reign of God should permeate our prayers and politics, our spirituality and sociality, how we relate with *God* and with others, shaping how we live in our homes and communities, what we contribute to the mission of the Church and to the common good of society. In sum, there is no nook or cranny of life, no time or place, where God is not to reign. Promoting a lived and living, whole and wholesome Christian faith toward God's reign is the ultimate purpose of catechetical education.

Effecting Total Catechetical Education

Not Any "Program" Alone

Given this sense of the nature and purpose of catechetical education, how then to do it effectively? What approach would best serve such a holistic description of Christian faith? Catechetical educators must always face the "how to" question, our focus for the remainder of this chapter.

Many times I've begun my graduate courses at Boston College by asking participants how education in faith is typically perceived in their culture. No matter where people come from or how they name it—catechesis, or religious education, or Christian religious education, or religious instruction, or Sunday school, or catechism, or whatever—the reigning stereotypes are fairly universal. A sample from a recent survey: children in a classroom learning about religion from a teacher; didactic instruction in religious knowledge; kids memorizing religious answers to questions they never ask; learning boring religion stuff that's supposed to become important someday; telling children how to be Christian; getting kids through the sacraments they should have; learning what Christians must believe, with no questions asked; or, a recent clincher, a one-hour, once-a-week drop off that should make y'er kids Christian.

Laughable but also sad. And note some of the consistencies: for children, teacher controlled, didactic, priority on information not personal appropriation, limited to some form of "schooling." Contemporary catechist-educators roundly reject all such stereotypes as does the current "mind" of the church, and yet we should be sobered by their tenacity. I suspect all of our thinking could still benefit from a bit of "de-schooling"; old ways die hard.

Educational reformer Ivan Illich made a controversial proposal some thirty years ago to "de-school society." He wanted to reverse the hand-over of education to schools as teacher-centered, ideologically controlled, and didactic places—for children only. Note well that Illich was not at all opposed to education; on the contrary, he wanted to save it from the hegemony of schooling that abstracts learning from life and voids the responsibilities of parents, homes, and communities. Illich would also caution that catechetical education must not be over-identified with "school" or "program" (the parish version of school). Of course, formal parish programs and parochial schools can play a significant role in faith education, but they should be no more than one feature of a total approach. In fact, I propose that we replace the didactic school paradigm with a sharing faith community.

Contrary to glib caricatures, and to restorationist nay-sayers, the church has made great progress in its catechetical ministry over the past one hundred years. Beginning with the Munich Method at the start of the twentieth century and Pope Pius X's insistence that young children be catechized for first eucharist, much ground has been gained. The GDC concurs: "Catechetical renewal, developed in the church over the last decades, continues to bear very welcome fruit" (no. 24). It also urges us to build upon this renewal and to break new ground. However, I've noticed a pervasive tendency to propose movements and approaches as total that, though worthy, are quite piecemeal. I even detect such "totalizing" in the GDC's enthusiasm for the catechumenate (more below). I don't believe any one program or approach will ever again be able—if one ever was—to provide the "permanent catechesis" required by every Christian person and community, from womb to tomb. So:

- The *program* or the *school* alone cannot fulfill all the church's responsibilities of catechetical education, although a parish program or parochial school with trained catechists and a curriculum of sound theology and good pedagogy are indispensable to education in Christian faith;

- The *parish* alone cannot do all catechetical education, though a vibrant faith community is vital, and every aspect of parish life should be intentionally crafted to educate in faith;

- The *family* alone cannot be the sole catechist, though it is ever the "first educator in faith" (ritual of baptism) and must harness every aspect of its life to nurture Christian identity and commitment;

- The *liturgy* alone cannot be the anchor for catechetical education, though likely nothing is more effective in fostering people's faith than good liturgy or more hazardous to faith than poor liturgy;

- The *lectionary* alone cannot provide the scope and sequence for the whole story of Christian faith, though lectionary-based curricula can encourage the correlation of liturgy and catechesis as well as inter-generational faith sharing, and help to recenter the Bible for Catholic Christians;

- The (published) *curriculum* alone cannot provide the complete guide to learning, though the texts and media used in formal catechetical education should reflect a thorough and theologically sound presentation of Christian faith and a pedagogy that actively engages participants in the teaching/learning dynamic;

- *Catechist-educators* alone cannot bear all responsibility for faith education, though well-informed and well-formed catechists who are credible witnesses to what they teach and who deepen their own spirituality are vital to educating in faith;

- The *catechumenate* alone cannot offer total preparation, although it is powerfully effective for initiating neophytes into Christian community and its values can inspire all catechetical education.

Here an expanded comment is in order, given the strong endorsement by the GDC of the catechumenal paradigm and what I perceive as an over-interpretation by enthusiasts of the RCIA. In what could be read as a "totalizing" move, the GDC proposes that "the model for all catechesis is the baptismal catechumenate" (no. 59). Though it recognizes that it is "non-baptized adults to whom the catechumenate truly and properly corresponds" (no. 172), yet the catechumenate's "inherent richness...should serve to inspire other forms of catechesis" (no. 68; see nos. 90–91). Here I encourage caution, emphasizing the word *inspire* and distinguishing between inspiration and imitation. Before my caveat, however, let me summarize some of the ways I believe the catechumenal model can inspire all instances of catechetical education.

The *Rite of Christian Initiation of Adults*, now considered "the ordinary catechumenate"[9] in the life of the church, does not recommend a particular pedagogy or approach to faith education.[10] It is literally a liturgical rite—in fact, a series of rites—celebrating four stages of initiation, from "pre-catechumenate," to "catechumenate," to "purification and illumination," to, after initiation, "a time of mystagogy" (no. 88). However, in the hands of some very creative leadership, the rite has called forth a pastoral practice that reflects the best of catechetical education. As such, what has emerged in the practice of the catechumenate can inspire all catechesis and religious education.

It reminds us:

- That Christian faith is for the whole person—head, heart, and hands—to be lived as discipleship to Jesus in every situation;

- That catechesis should inform, form, and transform people in Christian faith; it requires "integral formation rather than mere information" (no. 29);

- That Christian community is the primary context of catechetical education, advising that all the ministries of the parish be engaged to educate in faith, "catechesis is an essentially ecclesial act" (no. 78);

- That catechesis and liturgy are integrally related, each needing the other because ritual and sacred symbol are essential to pedagogy in faith, and, conversely, people must be educated for "full, conscious, and active participation"[11] in the liturgy;

- That catechesis must recenter the word of God through scripture at the core of Catholic faith as well as teaching tradition;

- That an hospitable community of people who reflect and share on God's presence in their lives, and encounter scripture and tradition in conversation together, is an effective pedagogy for educating in Christian faith.

Inspiring, indeed! But these principles reflect the best of contemporary catechetical education; there is no reason to designate them as *catechumenal*. To speak of catechumenal is to suggest stages of initiation.

It is fine to say, "But the catechumenate is more than its stages"; however, to exclude the stages is to describe something other than the catechumenate. And to impose the process of initiation on all catechesis—across the life span and even within families and contexts that are already Christian—seems contrived and ill-fitting, forcing square pegs into round holes.

For adult neophytes so initiated, the catechumenate has done its job; now something more is needed for "the maturing of initial conversion" (no. 82). And committed cradle Christians clearly need something more than an initiation process. That "more" should include good religious education that reaches beyond the socialization of the catechumenate. More inspiring than the GDC by way of such permanent catechesis for adults is the U.S. Catholic Bishops' statement *Our Hearts Were Burning Within Us*.[12] And see, too, Jane Regan's proposal in this collection for learning communities in an adult church.

For children in Christian families, why not simply encourage and empower parents to share their faith with their children, fostering their Christian identity from the first days of life? As Horace Bushnell advised over 150 years ago, rather than raising children for conversion as "a technical experience," better to nurture their faith from the beginning, so that they grow up Christians, never thinking of themselves otherwise.[13]

I honestly don't see how the stages of the catechumenate would help Christian parents to be more intentional about nurturing their children in faith—presuming that the children are already baptized. Of course, if parents have not raised their children as Christians, and the latter have reached the use of reason, then an adapted version of the catechumenate would be very appropriate for their initiation.[14] But in Christian families that should be the exception rather than the rule.

Indeed, I remember my mother addressing her brood of nine children on occasion as "a bunch of pagans" (as when no one remembered to say grace), but we presumed—or hoped—that this was not her defining estimation of us. Nor would her imaging herself as doing pre-catechumenate, purification, illumination, and mystagogy with us have enhanced her Christian parenting. Likewise, I do not see the catechumenal paradigm as an asset to address the generational politics of religious education that Thomas Beaudoin describes in his essay here.

The Broadest Coalition

Karl Rahner claimed that what revolutionized modern catechesis more than anything else was the redefinition of Christian faith effected by the Second Vatican Council. His point was that when faith was defined as *belief* in stated doctrines—the dominant sentiment of the Council of Trent (1545–63)—then catechesis could be done by a catechism that summarized beliefs and taught them clearly. Historically, it is true that easy-to-memorize question-and-answer catechisms did not emerge among Catholics until after Trent. But now that Christian faith has been reclaimed as a holistic way of life, as engaging head but also heart and hands, as demanding right belief but also right worship and right action, now something more is needed by way of catechetical education. Given such a total understanding of Christian faith, nothing less than *total catechetical education* will suffice.

Essentially, this is a shift beyond the "schooling didactic" paradigm to a "sharing faith community" one. Total catechetical education calls for:

- a coalition of family, parish, and program/school;

- involving all aspects of each—its whole communal life;

- engaging every member as both teacher and learner;

- across the life cycle from cradle to grave;

- in *sharing faith* together;

- as apprentices to Jesus for God's reign in the world.

This proposal entails a major shift in consciousness for Christians and their communities. For the person, the key shift is to see oneself as an educator in faith, ever being both learner and teacher of the Christian way, especially by living it. It calls for permanent catechesis as both sharer and receiver of Christian faith, always both catechist and catechized. On that hillside in Galilee when the Risen Christ gave the great commission—"Go, make disciples of all nations" (Matt 28:19)—he addressed all present. By baptism all Christians are to be agents of their faith, not simply dependents.

Two thousand years later the GDC states that catechesis is "an educational activity which arises from the particular responsibility of every member of the community" (no. 220). This should erase the line separating teachers and taught, encouraging the whole Christian community to become teachers and learners together—a sentiment proposed by Saint Thomas Aquinas some 750 years ago.

For every Christian community, total catechetical education requires catechetical consciousness in every aspect of its life. Social scientists tell us that human identity is formed, in large part, by our communal contexts; we become who we become through our relationships and socialization. Concomitantly, Christian faith is essentially communal. So, to live and grow in a communal faith surely requires the formative life of Christian communities—parish, family, and school or program. The GDC says that "the Christian community is the origin, locus, and goal of catechesis" (no. 245), and community includes "the family, parish, Catholic schools, Christian associations and movements, basic ecclesial communities" (no. 253).

So, total catechetical education means engaging every family, parish, and program/school to become Christian community and doing so with a "catechetical consciousness." This means asking of

19

every activity and effort, structure and arrangement, symbol and ritual, what is this teaching? It means harnessing every aspect of community life to encourage lived Christian faith. In other words, a Christian community must not limit faith education to its ministry of the word but should bring a catechetical intent to all its ministries. What might such total catechesis mean in practice?

All Ministries to Educate in Faith

We can outline the church's ministries in many ways. Since the earliest days, however, six Greek terms have had pride of place in naming the distinct functions of Christian ministry:

- *koinonia* (to be a life-giving community);
- *marturia* (to bear witness to Christian faith);
- *kerygma* (to evangelize and preach the good news);
- *didache* (to teach scripture and tradition);
- *leitourgia* (to worship as a community); and
- *diakonia* (to care for human needs).

I will summarize these in a fourfold schema (pairing *marturia* with *koinonia, didache* with *kerygma*) as the functions of *witness, worship, welfare* and *word*. I place *word* last because it is the obvious concern of faith education, whereas we need to raise catechetical consciousness around the other three. And let us imagine each being realized in the family, parish, and program/school.

The Whole Family as Catechetical Educator

The term *family* here goes beyond the nuclear image of two parents with two children to include extended and blended families;

20

single-, double-, and triple-parent families; in fact, *any bonded network of domestic life and nurture.* The Second Vatican Council reclaimed an ancient image of the family as "the domestic church."[15] This means that the family should intentionally participate in all the church's ministries, and, I'm proposing here, do so with a catechetical consciousness.

For educating in faith, the GDC emphasizes the ethos of the home. As "the primary agent of an *incarnate* transmission of faith" (no. 207), the family should provide a "positive and receptive environment" and the "explicit experience and practice of the faith" (no. 178). Rather than more formal didaction, family catechesis is "a Christian education more witnessed to than taught, more occasional than systematic, more on-going than structured into periods" (no. 255). A family's faith is more caught than taught; its communal life *is* its faith curriculum.

Family as *witness* means that the whole life of the home should be suffused with the values and perspectives of Christian faith. This requires that the members constantly review the family's environment and atmosphere, relationships and gender roles, lifestyle and patterns of living, work and recreation, to monitor how well the family reflects the convictions and commitments of Christian faith. In sum, everything about the Christian family should reflect and bear witness to its faith.

For a family to be a *worshipping* community, it needs to integrate shared prayer and sacred ritual into its patterns of daily life. Every Christian family needs its own "liturgy" to symbolize its faith. I once asked a devout Jewish friend how she came by her strong Jewish identity. She immediately responded, "Oh, from the rituals in my home." Surely every Christian family can create or rediscover—old Catholic cultures had plenty of them—sacred rituals for the home that will nurture and celebrate the Christian identity of its members. Without family liturgy, the home is less likely to educate in faith.

The family as agent of *welfare* requires care for the spiritual, physical, and emotional well-being of its own members, rippling out

21

to responsibility for others and society. Family life must realize love and compassion toward all, promoting justice within itself and the social values of God's reign in the world. If children grow up and adults dwell within a family that lives the values of mercy and compassion, of justice and peace, they are most likely to embrace the social responsibilities of Christian faith.

The family as a community of *word* shares its faith around scripture and tradition, within itself and in the broader community. Though continuing to participate in the formal programs of parishes and schools, every Christian should be "home-schooled." Parishes must empower parents—with resources, training, suggestions, support, encouragement, expectation—to share faith within the interactions of family life. I know a family that gathers every week for a family scripture moment. They read a passage from the Sunday lectionary and then each member shares what he or she heard from the text. Imagine the catechetical effect on both parents and children.

The Whole Parish as Catechetical Educator

The whole life of a parish community should be intentionally crafted to nurture the faith of its people. Every function of ministry should be done with a catechetical consciousness, that is, it should be deliberately crafted to educate in faith. Traditionally, we have thought of catechesis as a parish's ministry of the word. But we must bring a catechetical consciousness to *all* functions of ministry. The whole life of a parish is its faith curriculum; everything about it should make it a teaching/learning community.

To be a community of *witness*, a parish should reflect the good news it proclaims and be recognizable as a community of faith, hope and love. Beginning with Vatican II, official documents increasingly portray the church as God's "universal sacrament of salvation" (no. 45). Recall Aquinas's definition of a sacrament—a sacred symbol that causes what it symbolizes. As such, every parish should be effective in realizing what it preaches. Members must constantly ask: Does the life of this parish—its worship, shared prayer, and spiritual nurture; its community ethos, lifestyle, and structures; its human services, outreach, and social values; its preaching, catechesis, and sharing faith programs—bear credible witness to the way of Jesus? Is this community effective for the life of the world" (John 6:51)? To the extent that it can say yes, it is an effective catechetical educator.

Stating the obvious, every parish must assemble as a Christian people to *worship* God together. Often forgotten, however, is that this public work is likely to be the most educational function that a parish renders. Nothing educates in faith—or mis-educates—as effectively as a parish's liturgy.

For the majority of Christians, Sunday worship is their primary encounter with their faith community. The social sciences teach that a community shapes its people primarily through its symbols. Further, a people's sacred symbols are the most formative of all. In sum, then, the quality of a parish's liturgy is likely to be the measure of its effectiveness as an educator in faith.

Now, we must never forget that the primary function of liturgy is to worship God. To cite Vatican II, "The sacred liturgy is above all things the worship of the divine Majesty." So, liturgy must not be used to catechize in a didactic way; that would be an abuse of liturgy. On the other hand, precisely because it is so symbol-laden, the liturgy contains "abundant instruction for the faithful." Referring to all the sacraments, the council said: "Because they are signs they also instruct. They not only presuppose faith, but by words and objects they also nourish, strengthen, and express it."[16] So, it is likely that the most effective strategy for a parish to educate well is to care for the quality of its liturgy.

Every parish must be a community that cares for *human welfare*— spiritual and physical, personal and social. Living the way of Jesus demands the works of compassion and mercy, of justice and peace. The parish should offer people the inspiration and organization, the support and persuasion that prompt them to carry on this aspect of God's saving work in the world. *Diakonia* is required of Christians by their faith. My added point here, however, is that it's also required for the parish to be an effective catechist. When a parish has outreach to the poor and marginalized and participates in the social struggles for justice and peace, then it is likely to educate well in Christian faith.

Every parish must give its people ready access to the *word* of God that comes through the scriptures and tradition. The parish achieves this particularly through its preaching and formal programs of catechetical education. However, there are other ways of fulfilling the ministry of the word. I know of a parish that has copies of the Bible strewn throughout its whole plant, in every pew in church, every office, waiting room, meeting room, and parlor—even the stalls of the bathrooms have a Bible. Every gathering and committee meeting is encouraged to begin with a reading of the Sunday gospel and sharing by those present of "what I heard as a word of God for my life." This Catholic community places the Bible at the core of its faith; think of the educational effect!

The Whole School or Program as Catechetical Educator

By *school* here I include any church-sponsored school that educates in Christian faith. By *program* I mean any formal process of catechetical education—the graded parish curriculum for children and adolescents, all adult religious education, RCIA, youth ministry, faith-sharing groups, base communities, and so on. Together, school and program epitomize the church's intentional efforts to provide a formal curriculum of faith education. The point I emphasize, however, is that such catechetical education should not be limited to a ministry of the word—its most obvious purpose—but should integrate the other functions of ministry into its curriculum as well.

The whole environment of the school or program should *witness* to the values of a Christian community—respect and reverence for every person; hospitality and welcome toward all; and faith, hope, and love. Years ago John Dewey argued convincingly that schools should reflect the values of a democratic society—if they intend to educate people for democracy. Surely we can say as much of a Christian school or parish program, that it should be suffused with the values and commitments of Christian faith. Further, catechetical education should encourage participants to be active in their local Christian community, nurturing their ecclesial identity.

Opportunities for shared prayer and *worship*, for spiritual experiences like retreats and discernment, should be integral to the curriculum of every school or program. This is not to say that the Catholic school or program should replace the parish in its ministry of worship. But the very pedagogy of a class or gathering can include moments of prayer and contemplation, of ritual and celebration—within the teaching/learning dynamic. I know of a parish program that designates its grade-level gatherings as Christian communities instead of classes. Each one chooses an inspiring name for itself and has its own rituals for praying together and celebrating the liturgical year—Advent wreaths, Christmas plays, Lenten fasts, Easter celebrations, and so on.

For the program or school to be a community of *welfare*, the Thanksgiving baskets or visits to the local rest home or serving at a soup kitchen are not an add-on to the formal curriculum but integral to it. In fact, the whole pedagogy employed should entail an invitation to decision for lived Christian faith. And when corporate decisions are made, there should be opportunities within the catechetical program to carry them out, for example, through works of compassion and mercy, justice and peace.

The most obvious purpose of the school or program is as ministry of the *word*. To echo earlier reflections, however, this cannot be fulfilled by programs of "informing" alone, as if enabling people to "know about" their faith is sufficient. Rather, the informing—study, instruction, and conversation—should be done in a way that is likely to form and transform people as well, to nurture their hearts and hands in addition to their heads in the wisdom of Christian faith. I turn now to sketch a pedagogy that seems appropriate to such holistic intent.

God's Pedagogy as Our Own

Total catechetical education engages every member and all aspects of every Christian community in sharing faith together. So, all Christian persons and communities are called to a catechetical consciousness that permeates their whole way of being in the world, ever teaching and learning for lived Christian faith. This is the "sharing faith community" paradigm of catechetical education.

Then, within this comprehensive umbrella, we need an effective and appropriate pedagogy—an intentional way of structuring teaching/learning events. Such pedagogy should be capable of honoring the values of catechesis and religious education. This means that it should nurture people's Christian identity with a thorough knowledge of their faith and, conversely, teach the wisdom of Christian story in ways likely to form faith identity.

Regarding pedagogy, the GDC makes a rather amazing proposal, and, perhaps, its most memorable one. It proposes that "the pedagogy of God," which is also reflected in "the pedagogy of Jesus," should be "the source and model of the pedagogy of faith" by Christians.[17] At the end of this lengthy essay, I can only extrapolate and summarize.

God enters into and is actively present through the events of human history. Thus, history is the locus of God's self-disclosure. Over time, and guided by the Holy Spirit, the great scriptures and traditions of Christian faith emerged from communities reflecting upon their experiences of God's presence and saving deeds, climaxing for Christians in the life of Jesus Christ. Now, people can inherit this "faith handed down" by learning the scriptures and traditions that mediate this normative revelation. However, if people are to appropriate Christian faith as their own, then pedagogy now should reflect God's pedagogy over time. This proposal has at least three implications.

First, the teaching/learning dynamic must be an active and participative one; a docile reception of "the faith" is not sufficient. So, catechetical education should "promote active participation among those to be catechized" (no. 145) and encourage "dialogue and sharing" (no. 159) among participants. Likewise, every participant "must be an active subject, conscious and co-responsible, and not merely a silent and passive recipient" (no. 167). The rationale for this is both anthropological and theological: "The active participation of all the catechized in their formative process is completely in harmony, not only with genuine human communication, but specifically with the economy of Revelation and salvation" (no. 157). Clearly, what Paulo Freire condemned as "banking education"—depositing information in passive receptacles—is also unworthy of catechetical education.

Second, the teaching dynamic must draw upon the experiences and lives of participants as integral to the curriculum. The GDC reiterates this point repeatedly. For example: "Catechesis is...realized in the encounter of the word of God with the experience of the person" (no. 150); "experience is a necessary medium for exploring and assimilating the truths which constitute the objective content of Revelation" (no. 152b); "The catechist must teach the person to read his own lived experience" because experience is "the locus" of "the pedagogy of the Incarnation" (no. 152c).

Third, the core dynamic of catechetical pedagogy is to teach the faith tradition *through* and *for* people's lives. This means bringing together and integrating people's lives with the faith handed down, merging life and Christian faith into living faith. Thus, catechetical pedagogy should encourage "a correlation and interaction between profound human experiences and the revealed message" (no. 153). Again, "Catechesis...bridges the gap between belief and life, between the Christian message and the cultural context" (no. 205); it ever intends "to link...orthodoxy and orthopraxis" (no. 237), "correlating faith and life" (no. 207).

Over many years, my own work has attempted to articulate a shared Christian praxis approach to catechesis and religious education. The ideal context of this approach is a community of conversation and active participation by all in sharing faith together. It typically unfolds as a process of bringing life to faith and bringing faith to life. It invites people to look at and reflect on their lives together, to bring this praxis to encounter, to reflect upon and to learn the wisdom of Christian story, and then to make this faith their own, appropriating and choosing to live it as faith alive in the world.[18]

Far from separating catechesis and religious education, such a pedagogy bonds them as one—catechetical education. As a communal process, it is eminently suited to the paradigm of total catechetical education. And by God's grace working through some such paradigm and pedagogy, the Christian community will continue its "pilgrim's progress" into the vision of God's reign.

Notes

1. Avery Dulles, "John Paul and the New Evangelization," *America* (1 February 1992), 52.
2. Ibid, 53.
3. See "Decree on the Church's Missionary Activity," in Abbot, *Documents of Vatican II* (New York: America Press) 590–93, no. 6.
4. Pope Paul VI, "On the Evangelization of Peoples" (Washington, D.C.: USCC, 1975), nos. 18, 9.
5. "Decree on the Church's Missionary Activity," in Abbott, *Documents of Vatican II*, 598, no. 11.
6. "Declaration on the Relationship of the Church to Non-Christian Religions," in Abbott, *Documents of Vatican II*, 662, no. 2.
7. Ibid, 663.
8. *The Catechism of the Catholic Church* (New York: W.H. Sadlier, 1994) no. 780.

9. Ibid, no. 18.

10. Some of the great pathfinders in implementing the RCIA, like Fr. James Dunning and Christiane Brusselmans—God rest them both—footnoted my own work on a "shared praxis approach" as influencing the pedagogy they proposed for catechumenal catechesis..

11. "Constitution on the Sacred Liturgy," in Abbott, *Documents of Vatican II*, 144, no. 14.

12. *Our Hearts Were Burning Within Us* (Washington, D.C.: USCC, 1999).

13. See Horace Bushnell, *Christian Nurture* (New Haven, Conn.: Yale Univ. Press, 1947), 4.

14. "Since children who have reached the use of reason are considered, for purposes of Christian initiation, to be adults (canon 852.1), their formation should follow the ordinary catechumenate as far as possible, with the appropriate adaptations permitted by the ritual" (*Rite of Christian Initiation of Adults*, no. 18).

15. "Dogmatic Constitution on the Church," in Abbott, *Documents of Vatican II*, no. 11.

16. "Constitution on the Sacred Liturgy," in Abbott, *Documents of Vatican II*, nos. 33, 59.

17. See all of Part Three of the GDC, esp. chap. I, nos. 139–47.

18. For a complete statement of a shared praxis approach, see Thomas Groome, *Sharing Faith* (Portland, Oreg.: Wipf and Stock, 1998).

2

The Aim of Catechesis: Educating for an Adult Church

Jane E. Regan

The story is told of an artist, marooned on an island for years. Her prized possession is a sculpture that she has spent years creating from bits of metal found on the island. In the process of shaping this work, she has grown in her understanding of the sculpting process, of herself, and of the way in which art gives expression to beauty and to truth. Although she is very proud of her creation, she also realizes that she has grown beyond it—both as an artist and as a person. She is confident that her next work of art will express new depth and challenge her even further in her work and in her life.

So she goes in search of more metal. She scours the island and is disappointed to discover that there is no more metal to be found. She realizes that she can only give expression to her new insights, her new creative movements by melting down and remolding the first creation.

How does this story end? Perhaps the artist simply cannot face the pain of dismantling the first work in which so much energy and creativity and imagination had been invested over the years. And so she continues to tinker with the first sculpture: adding some elements, shoring up others.

Or, perhaps, she gazes on the sculpture with gratitude for new insights and new understandings, and after a poignant pause, she turns to light the fire.[1]

In some ways this parable points to what I think these times are about in the catechetical enterprise. We have a structure, created and carefully shaped over the last fifty to sixty years. Like a communal sculptor, we each have added and enhanced the edifice of religious education as it has come to expression in parishes across the country and around the world. We have learned much in the process. And, while there is much good to be said about the present structure, we recognize elements of the creation that have grown out of proportion to the overall sculpture. There are sections we have returned to regularly, and yet they have not evolved in the way we had hoped. And there are still other elements that seem to be all but totally disconnected from the larger creation.

So what do we do? Do we continue to tinker with the present sculpture—aware of its strengths and weaknesses—or do we light the fire for a new sculpture? I propose a reorienting of the catechetical enterprise to create a new sculpture. To light the fire for the new creation, I suggest we begin by exploring evangelization as the central task of the church. Such an exploration can lead to a renewed understanding of the work of catechesis as essential to the life of the church, the importance of ongoing and lifelong faith formation, and the catechesis of adults as the chief form of catechesis.

Building upon an understanding of evangelization, I suggest we remold the sculpture of catechesis so that it becomes evangelizing catechesis within the parish as a learning community. For parishes to embrace evangelization as central to catechesis, they must become learning communities, always open to and fostering a deepening of faith and a continual reshaping of Christian beliefs and practices to address the signs of the times. As Christian believers are formed in faith, they, in turn, can become evangelizers. On a corporate level, a parish can become a vibrant evangelizing community able to foster and enrich the faith life of children and youth while at the same time reaching out to those beyond the boundaries of the community.

To examine this more closely, this chapter considers three questions: (1) What are the implications for speaking about adult formation in the context of evangelization? (2) How do we move away from a focus on simply establishing programs for adults and move toward forming a learning community? (3) What are the implications of bringing the concepts of evangelization and learning communities into dialogue around the topic of adult faith formation?[2]

Adult Formation in the Context of Evangelization

I recommend that we take adult faith formation much more seriously than we have in the past. When this is viewed through the filter of our existing paradigm of catechesis, I might be heard as suggesting the need to set up more faith-formation programs for adults. Actually, I propose something much more radical. To understand what I am recommending, we need to name more clearly what we mean by evangelization.

This call to evangelization reflects a renewed commitment to the key imperative that the disciples heard and came to own as they grappled with taking on new roles and new responsibilities in post-resurrection times. They, like we, came to understand themselves as living in the interim time between Jesus' coming in history and the final coming—the fulfillment of all human hope. It is in that context that they understood the post-resurrection proclamation at the end of Matthew's gospel:

> Full authority has been given to me both in heaven and on earth; go therefore and make disciples of all the nations. Baptize them in the name of the Father and of the Son and of the Holy Spirit. Teach them to carry out everything I

have commanded you. And know that I will be with you always, until the end of the world. (Matt 28: 18–20)

This is the heart of the call to evangelization that we all inherit by virtue of baptism.

In the first essay of this collection, Thomas Groome highlights the importance of the shift in our understanding of evangelization that has taken place in the years since Vatican Council II. He makes clear that the way in which the *General Directory for Catechesis* (GDC) speaks of evangelization is far different from the "Catholic stereotype of evangelization—as conversion."[3] One way to speak about this is to name the difference between proselytizing and evangelizing.

In the case of proselytizing, the believer is primarily engaged in preaching, with the message focused on telling the other what to believe.[4] In the case of evangelizing, the believer is engaged in giving expression to his or her beliefs in all of the day-to-day activities that shape life. When words are called for, the believer talks about what he or she believes rather than telling the other what to believe. Often, those who don't share in the faith convictions of the believer experience proselytizing as oppressive. One of the surest signs of evangelization is that it is instead experienced as liberating. The goal of proselytizing is bringing in new members; the goal of evangelizing is the furthering of the reign of God, "bringing the Good News into all the strata of humanity, and through its influence transforming humanity from within and making it new."[5]

Fundamentally, evangelization has to do with how the parish lives and makes all of its decisions: how to spend money, how to allocate time and space, how to respond to the needs of people both within and outside the community of faith, how to address the social structures that support or take away from human living.

Seeing that evangelization is as much about who we are as what we do, it might be helpful to think not only of the noun *evangelization* but of the descriptor *evangelizing* as well. When we use the term *evangelization*, there is the temptation to set it out as another activity the parish does—catechesis, liturgy, pastoral care, evangelization—or to see it as the responsibility of a single committee—the evangelization committee—similar to the other committees a parish might have, such as the social committee, the school committee, or the budget committee. Using the descriptor *evangelizing* strengthens the commitment that who we are as church, our mission and identity, is rooted in our engaging in all activities through the lens of evangelization. To claim that we are an evangelizing community means that we have the responsibility of bringing the word of God into every dimension of human life. Evangelization brings us beyond the boundaries of parochial life and requires that we recognize that all action, both corporate and individual, must have the goal of furthering the reign of God and enhancing a context of justice.

To speak of "evangelizing pastoral care," for example, reminds us that as we visit the sick, as we care for the bereaved or lonely, as we counsel the lost or confused, we do these activities in a way that recognizes the close connection between human life and the liberating word of Jesus Christ. We do all of these activities to proclaim the gospel in word and action and thus further the reign of God. And so we can speak of evangelizing youth ministry, evangelizing liturgy, and even evangelizing budget committee.

It is in this sense that we speak of *evangelizing catechesis*, naming catechesis as a moment of evangelization, "an essential and remarkable one" (GDC, no. 63). Situating catechesis within the work of evangelization has significant implications for how we perceive and engage in the catechetical enterprise.

First, recognizing the foundational connection between evangelization and catechesis means moving the work of catechesis to a central place in the life of the church and seeing it as essential to the church's ability to live out its mission.

Second, the relationship of catechesis to evangelization also adds clarity to the task of catechesis. The relationship of evangelization and catechesis is twofold. From one perspective we can speak of the relationship between evangelization and catechesis in terms of the movement of the person from first hearing the gospel, to initial conversion to Jesus Christ, to a participation in catechesis toward initiation. That is the general dynamic of what we see presented in the GDC as initiatory or baptismal catechesis. This movement from evangelization to catechesis leads to an individual committed to Jesus Christ and formed in the ways and teachings of the Christian community. So what we are about in catechesis is conversion and entering into a discipleship that lasts a lifetime and calls for continuing formation and transformation in terms of ongoing catechesis.

But the relationship between evangelization and catechesis goes beyond simply initiating and socializing new members; catechesis is at the heart of the process whereby the person who had been evangelized becomes an evangelizer. Through catechesis the parish is formed and transformed into an evangelizing community. The movement then is not simply from evangelization to catechesis but also from catechesis to evangelization.

In light of this, we can speak about a third implication of looking at catechesis through the lens of evangelization: It provides a clear vision for where we are to place the focus of the catechetical work. There is a way in which the lens of evangelization makes meaningful statements that have been appearing in catechetical documents since the first GDC in 1971: "Catechesis of adults, since it deals with persons who are capable of an adherence that is fully responsible must be considered the chief form of catechesis. All the other forms, which are indeed always necessary, are in some way oriented to it" (no. 20). If we understand that what we are about is forming an evangelizing church, the focus has to be adult faith formation—not in an exclusive way but in a radical way.

Adult Catechesis in the Christian Community (ACCC) says this with profound clarity:

In summary, in order for the Good News of the Kingdom to penetrate all the various layers of the human family, it is crucial that every Christian play an active part in the coming of the Kingdom....All of this naturally requires adults to play a primary role. Hence it is not only legitimate, but necessary to acknowledge that a fully Christian community can only exist when a systematic catechesis of all its members takes place and when an effective and well-developed catechesis of adults is regarded as the *central task* in the catechetical enterprise. (ACCC, no. 25)[6]

So, to speak of evangelizing catechesis clarifies the place of catechesis at the heart of the mission of the church. It makes clear that we are about forming an evangelizing community; and it heightens our awareness that our focus is on adults, recognizing that doing this serves in the formation of a dynamic, vibrant community that is able to foster and enrich the faith life of children and youth.

Parish as Learning Community

The close relationship between catechesis and evangelization and the nature of evangelizing catechesis teaches us that our attention must be focused first on the adult community. When we make that affirmation—one that has been made by catechetical documents and many catechetical leaders over the past thirty-five years—we too often deal with it in programmatic ways. We ask about more programs, better programs, programs following explicitly articulated adult-learning models. We search for texts or speakers or approaches that will engage, entice, and enliven the adults within our setting. My proposal here is that we not look only for a new program but, more important, for a new perspective. The question is this: What would be the effect of seeing that what we are to do is form our parishes and our dioceses as *learning communities?*

In this, I am picking up an image developed within business circles, the concept of a learning organization.[7] We tend to toss around phrases like *learning community* with some ease, but the term *learning organization* is understood in a fairly formal way within the literature from the business sector. In that context, there is a good deal of conversation about the need for companies and business of all sorts to be and to become learning organizations. Of course, we must be careful when taking insights from one discipline (business) and applying them in another (catechetics). Still, it raises some interesting ideas that are well worth our consideration.

Three questions can guide our thinking on the concept of learning communities: (1) It is clear why schools and parishes or congregations might find it helpful to understand themselves as learning communities/organizations, but why are businesses seeing that necessity? (2) What are the characteristics of a learning community/organization and how does that go beyond simply offering good programs for adults? (3) What are the implications of this for how we think about the reality of adult faith formation within our pastoral settings?

Learning Organizations—"Learning at the Speed of Change"

We are all familiar with the kind of past-present comparisons that remind us of what we already know: The way in which change has taken place and the rate of change within Western culture, and specifically within the United States context, is noteworthy. Increasing mobility has resulted in fewer people living within an easy drive of their home of origin. The percentage of families headed by a married couple is decreasing, while families headed by single women are increasing, and that does not even address the situation of blended families. The work force is also in a constant state of change. While word of low unemployment at the beginning of the twenty-first century sounds promising, the reality does not always match.

Less positive elements include the lack of job security and the necessity of more than one job to cover the expenses of an average family.

These kind of sociological and demographic realities point to a
shift in our understanding of the dialectic between stability and
change. The adage that the only thing that is certain is change has
become so obvious that we hardly attend. So, for businesses and
organizations, the reality of change and the speed of change means
that to survive and thrive, there must be an openness to seeing the
future and creating the future in a new way.[8]

One common way to think and talk about this kind of change is
to speak of a *paradigm shift,* a concept introduced to the scientific
world by Thomas Kuhn and clarified by those who came after him.[9]
Willis Haram provides this helpful definition:

A paradigm is the basic way of perceiving, thinking, valu-
ing, and doing associated with a particular vision of reality. A dominant paradigm is seldom if ever stated
explicitly; it exists as unquestioned, tacit understanding
that is transmitted through culture and to succeeding generations through direct experience rather than taught.[10]

One of the classic examples of the effect of a dominant paradigm and of a paradigm shift can be found in considering the fortunes
of the Swiss watchmakers. From holding the majority market share of
the world's watches and having thousands of people employed as
watchmakers, the Swiss moved in fewer than ten years to having a
very small share of the world's watch market and hundreds of Swiss
watchmakers out of work.[11] The majority of the Swiss market share
went to the Japanese. What happened? This fundamental change can
be traced to the introduction of the quartz movement watch. The
quartz watch totally shifted the rules of watchmaking and the very
definition of watches. It challenged the dominant watch paradigm.

With the introduction of the quartz watch, all of the skills and abilities of the watchmakers of old could not prevent the shift.

The ironic piece to this story is that it was Swiss research-and-development people who invented the new quartz watch. But when they showed it to their own company management, it was rejected because it didn't look and work like a watch they knew. They were so sure of their old paradigm of what a watch was that they did not even patent it. When they put it on display at an international watch fair, it was spotted by Texas Instrument and Seiko, and the rest is history. In telling this story, Joel Barker draws this conclusion:

> They were blinded by the success of their old paradigm and all their investment in it. And when confronted with a profoundly new and different way to continue their success into the future, they rejected it because it didn't fit the rules they were already so good at.[12]

Barker goes on to say that one of the rules of paradigms is that with a new paradigm, everyone goes back to zero—the rules for success have changed and the old way is simply not effective.

So, no matter what terminology is used, change happens, radical change that alters rules and boundaries. The organizations that will survive and thrive are those that can redefine and remake their future in the context of this rapid change. To do this, there needs to be a means within the organization or community for tapping into the energy and insights of all involved and drawing on those insights to create a new future. This is at the heart of the learning organization. According to Peter Senge, a major voice in the formation of learning communities, "[t]his then is the basic meaning of a 'learning organization'—an organization that is continually expanding its capacity to create its future."[13]

So, why do business and other organizations want to be about learning? Because it is only through learning that they can continue to achieve their goals and vision. Hospitals, social-service agencies, insurance companies, bookstores, retail stores of all kinds—all of these have learned to be learning organizations in order to survive.

Now, what does this have to do with the work of a catechetical leader? Here are three scenarios that give some sense of the importance of understanding the reality of change and the necessity that our parishes and our dioceses become learning communities.

An announcement is made by the local bishop that over the next five years, ten parishes are going to be closed or merged. You are the DRE in a small and aging parish, and you realize that even if your parish is not closed, there will be ways in which your parish will be affected by the announcement. And you know that in some way the parish needs to redefine its vision and identity in order to survive, not necessarily as an incorporated parish but as a community of faith.

After one too many problems with the city officials, the main "soup kitchen" in your area of the city has closed. This means that literally hundreds of people will be without food or will be forced to travel to another part of the city for meals; for many that is impossible. The school that is part of your parish closed a couple of years ago and the building was converted into offices, meeting spaces and rooms for catechesis. The least used part of the building is the kitchen and cafeteria, and you are thinking that hosting a free lunch in that space, even just a couple times a week, might well serve the needs of some of those who are affected by the soup kitchen's closing. This differs significantly from the way most parishioners think the building should be used.

The deliberation of the local hospital ethics board hits the newspaper with a controversial decision regarding end of life issues. It has become an interesting and sometimes heated conversation among the elders who attend daily liturgy. Still, the conversation seldom gets beyond each person's opinion, and while those opinions are important there is the entire Christian tradition to consider and the wider conversation of the community to engage. But there are no forums in place to do that.

These are the fundamental questions of adult faith formation. This is the kind of rapid change that our parishes and parishioners are experiencing and to which we need to respond effectively in order to be true to our evangelizing mission. The capacity to engage these questions is at the heart of being a learning community. But beyond the pragmatic reason for shaping our parish toward becoming learning communities, that is, so that we can respond effectively to the reality of change, there are core theological foundations for such a revisioning.

Here is one way to think about it: By virtue of baptism, all Christians receive the presence of the Holy Spirit and the call to be active participants in building up the body of Christ and furthering the mission of the church. Through initiation all members receive gifts that are given for the good of the community, and it is incumbent on the leadership and the membership that these gifts be put to good use. Our ecclesiology, which arises from our understanding of the work of the Holy Spirit, affirms that wisdom and insight rest not merely with the designated leaders but within the life of the church as lived by all. So we work to foster genuine Christian learning communities not only as a practical way of effectively addressing rapid change but also because of the defining conviction that the Spirit is alive and active in all members of the community of faith.

Jane E. Regan

Characteristics of a Learning Community

There is a good deal of literature on this topic. As a way of synthesizing the voices of researchers such as Peter Senge, who examines the nature and function of learning organizations, and Thomas Hawkins, who brings this theory into conversation with the reality of the faith community, I set out here three characteristics of a learning community that I think have particular importance for the Christian community.

1. *A learning community maintains a clearly defined vision of its fundamental identity.* A clearly defined vision serves as an essential source of motivation for learning of all sorts. Homeowners decide to improve the appearance and value of their home, so they set out to learn what they can about landscaping and gardening. Parents, realizing that their child has a learning disability, gather information and insights in order to move toward the goal of obtaining the best and most appropriate education for their child. With a clear vision guiding our lives and decisions, we are motivated to learn all that is necessary to live into that vision. When a community has an articulated vision, one that is known and owned within the various segments of the group, there is a common motivation to engage in the learning—critical reflection and conversations—that serves to bring this vision to light.

Within the context of adult faith formation, and in the life of the parish in general, the vision is shaped by our understanding of evangelization as the fundamental mission of the church. On one level this serves as a major criteria for planning and implementing programs in the area of adult faith formation: Does this further the fundamental vision of this faith community as an evangelizing church? At the same time it serves to motivate us and those with whom we work to develop continually the knowledge, skills, and attitudes that contribute to our engaging effectively with adults. So, to speak of a parish as learning community means first being clear of the guiding vision and articulating that vision consistently and with clarity.

2. *Within a learning community genuine learning is fostered and supported at all levels.* A few years back I was living in the Midwest and was part of a parish that made the decision to shift from a child-centered to an adult-centered process of faith formation. The transition actually went fairly smoothly, and now, some ten years later, the parish continues to have a vibrant process of faith formation for all members of the parish. When the approach was first put in place and people from other parishes asked how long it had taken to implement, two answers were given. The short answer was that the decision was made in April and the new program was up and running in September. But the long answer gives some indication of the foundation upon which the program was built; that is, for many years, the parish had been moving toward being a learning community.

This learning community perspective was evident in many ways. Most of the committee meetings and gathering of ministers included some sort of formative experience. When the lector schedule was mailed out, there was an article enclosed that connected in some way with the liturgical season or contemporary scripture study. If one had an appointment with a member of the staff, the waiting area included a wide array of current periodicals—*America* or *Commonweal* or *U.S. Catholic*. When the parish needed to make the decision to build a parish center, everyone was invited and encouraged to be engaged in the process. Bulletin inserts regularly articulated the differing opinions and perspectives of those within the parish. Opportunities for extended conversation around the core issues were provided. In a wide variety of ways the ambiance of the parish was shaped by the presumption that everyone at every level was involved in learning.

3. *A learning community engages in system thinking, recognizing the dynamic complexity of the community and community learning.* For Peter Senge, this is a fundamental characteristic of a learning organization. He writes: "Systems thinking is a discipline for seeing wholes. It is a

framework for seeing interrelationships rather than things, for seeing patterns of change rather than static 'snapshots.'"[14]

At its most foundational systems thinking means recognizing that faith formation happens in contexts extending far beyond any formal programs. The process of growth in faith of any individual and any community is complex and multifaceted. The more clearly we recognize and embrace the multiple ways in which people and communities grow in faith, the more effective our work will be. Not only is no single approach the answer, but no particular dimension of parish life by itself can fashion the parish into a learning community.

To approach the parish as learning community from the perspective of systems thinking involves moving away from a "silo" approach to parish life. In many contexts the various aspects of the parish—youth ministry, liturgy, school, action for justice, religious education, and so on—are seen as discrete units of the whole; they exist side by side but without much interaction. Systems thinking invites and even requires that the interconnection among the various aspects and dimensions of parish life be recognized and that all the gifts of all the people be utilized.

Central to systems thinking is the notion of a dynamic complexity within which cause-and-effect relationships are not always clear. Senge writes: "When the same action has dramatically different effects in the short run and the long, there is dynamic complexity."[15] While making sessions for parents of children in the Eucharist program mandatory may in the short term lead to more adults attending, the long-term effect works against the recognition of the role of adult learners in their own learning/formation. While engaging and entertaining speakers with "package presentations" may in the short run provide for an enjoyable evening, the lack of opportunity for adults to engage with one another around issues of faith leads to a diminishment of the ongoing task of bringing faith into dialogue with life. Taking time to study a document in a parish committee in the short run means that not as much seems to be getting done, but the long-term impact is to contribute to the creation of a learning community that more effectively engages everyone's ideas and insights into the work of the committee. In each of these contexts the dynamic complexity of the learning community requires that we continually rearticulate our vision and respond in a way that furthers it.

Evangelization and Learning Community in Dialogue: Implications

As we bring our understanding of evangelization as the fundamental context for *understanding* catechesis into dialogue with learning community as the fundamental context for *doing* catechesis, several significant implications come to light. Let me here simply name and briefly describe four of them.[16]

1. *Adult faith formation within the parish as learning community is an integral part of parish life at all levels.* This is almost the definition of a learning community. The separation of catechesis from other elements of parish life—liturgy, social justice, school, youth ministry—is simply untenable in this context. The GDC makes clear that the cooperation and coordination of ministries of faith formation is not simply for efficiency but is itself a witness of the call for unity and has an effect on the church's ability to evangelize.[17]

Given the cultural dynamics outlined by Harold Horell and Tom Beaudoin in their essays in this collection, the need for ongoing formation for all members of the parish community is essential. Horell writes, "As the pace of cultural change accelerates, we must also recognize the need for ongoing faith formation that enables us to relate our Christian faith to the complexities and ambiguities of our everchanging postmodern world."

What this is calling for is not simply an ad hoc collection of presentations offered at various times in response to specified needs or desires, though certainly opportunities to examine specific concerns and events within the context of the Christian community is an essential element of the Christian's ability to respond to the events of the day. In addition, we need to establish ways of being community and engaging in the life and work of the church that support our involvement in the mission of the church, which brings the second implication into focus.

2. *Structures are created within the parish that provide space for genuine conversation among adults.* It is here, in the structuring of opportunities for adults to gather for conversation about things that matter, that the work of evangelization and the hope for a learning community come together. How do we shape our parishes into evangelizing, learning communities? A core element of the response must be to give adults the opportunity, support, and impetus to talk with other adults about the way in which faith and life intersect for them.

This is actually a two-step process. First, we consider all of the times and settings in which adults gather within a faith context: meeting of the lectors, social gathering after Sunday liturgy, choir practice, and so on. We can draw on these times as opportunities to enhance the faith and not simply the formation for ministry. Second, we set up times and settings conducive to adult conversation. Too often, once the programs for children and youth are scheduled and set, there is little time or appropriate space for adults to gather. Setting structures for adult conversation is essential.

3. *The wisdom of all members of the parish community is consistently recognized and affirmed.* Learning communities thrive when the insight and perspective and experience of a broad base of the community are accessed and respected. To do this, a spirit of mutuality and collaboration serves as the foundation. The community gathers, not divided between those "in the know" and the "folks in the pew" but as people who are attempting to journey together toward being a more effective evangelizing force.

While Tom Beaudoin makes a compelling case for the importance of structuring opportunities for faith formation for young adults, it would be helpful and important to name the ways in which the rest of the community can learn from the wisdom of the post–Vatican II generations, particularly when a good percentage of ecclesial leadership is adults who came to religious consciousness before or during the Second Vatican Council. Recognizing the wisdom of *all* members of the community is essential.

4. *The overarching goal of adult faith formation is to foster a sense of mission rather than simply to enhance membership.* At its most integral, adult catechesis provides participants with the means and perspectives that allow them to give expression to their baptism through engagement with the mission of evangelization. Behind this capacity to be an evangelizing community is the fundamental goal of catechesis to educate for spiritual maturity. As Colleen Griffith writes in this collection: "To identify spiritual maturity as the purpose of catechetical activity is to make relational life with God, and love for humanity and the world one's primary focus."

While we want and encourage an active sense of membership expressed in service to the community of faith, ultimately, the church is gathered to be sent, and the most important expression of the reality of the church is its commitment to transform the world in light of the reign of God. The work of evangelization is at the heart of the church's mission and the fundamental direction of the catechetical enterprise. To do this we are called to maintain a focus on ongoing spiritual maturity that has the capacity to respond to cultural realities and the needs of all humanity for a message of peace and justice. This is the work that we are about: total catechetical education for the sake of the reign of God.

Notes

1. Adapted from a story presented in Thomas R. Hawkins, *The Learning Congregation: A New Vision of Leadership* (Louisville, Ky.: Westminster John Knox Press, 1997), 33–34.
2. The conversations and questions explored with colleagues and participants at the National Symposium on the Future of Religious Education

at Boston College, 9–14 July 2000 enhanced my engagement with many of the issues examined in this chapter.

3. See Thomas Groome's discussion of the five developments of an understanding of evangelization in his essay in this collection.

4. I write on this distinction and the history of the shift in the understanding of evangelization in "Chapter 1 Toward an Adult Church," in *Toward an Adult Church: A Vision of Faith Formation* (Chicago: Loyola, 2002).

5. Pope Paul VI, *On Evangelization in the Modern World (Evangelii Nuntiandi)* (1975), no. 18. Reprinted in *The Catechetical Documents: A Parish Resource*, ed. Martin Connell (Chicago: Liturgy Training Publications, 1996).

6. International Council for Catechesis, *Adult Catechesis in the Christian Community: Some Principles and Guidelines, with Discussion Guide* (Washington, D.C.: United States Catholic Conference, 1992).

7. One of the primary voices to set out the notion of learning organizations is Peter Senge. In *The Fifth Discipline: The Art and Practice of the Learning Organization* (New York: Doubleday/Currency, 1990), Senge examines the five disciplines of the learning organization: personal mastery, mental models, shared vision, team learning, and systems thinking. The other primary book by Senge is *The Fifth Discipline Fieldbook: Strategies and Tools for Building a Learning Organization* (New York: Currency, 1994). A collection of essays examining various elements of concepts related to the role of community building and learning organization can be found in Kaximierz Gozdz, ed., *Community Building: Renewing Spirit and Learning in Business* (San Francisco: New Leaders Press, 1995). For a review of the early literature of learning organizations, see Sandra Kerka, "The Learning Organization," in *Myths and Realities* (Columbus, Ohio: ERIC Clearinghouse on Adult, Career and Vocational Education, 1995). Kerka makes the important point that while a learning organization as an ideal is a helpful construct, it is a state that is never fully achieved. A more extensive discussion of the concept of learning organizations as a way of moving toward a learning society can be found in Victoria Marsick, Jeanne Bitterman, and Ruud van der Veen, "From the Learning Organization to Learning Communities Toward a Learning Society," in *Information Series No. 382* (Columbus, Ohio: ERIC Clearinghouse on Adult, Career and Vocational Education, 2000).

8. Throughout this section I follow the movement set out by Hawkins in *The Learning Congregation*. The first part of his book highlights the challenge of change and the way in which this has affected the way in which we live and learn. The heart of his argument is that the necessity for becoming a learning community is rooted in the rapidity of change at all levels of society and culture.

9. Thomas S. Kuhn, *The Structure of Scientific Revolutions, International Encyclopedia of Unified Science: Foundations of the Unity of Science*, vol. 2, no. 2 (Chicago: University of Chicago Press, 1962).

10. Willis Haram, *An Incomplete Guide to the Future* (New York: W. W. Norton, 1976).

11. Joel Arthus Barker, *Paradigms: The Business of Discovering the Future* (New York: HarperBusiness, 1993).

12. Ibid.

13. Senge, *The Fifth Discipline: The Art and Practice of the Learning Organization*, 14.

14. Ibid., 68.

15. Ibid., 71.

16. These ideas are developed a bit more in my essay "When Is Catechesis of Adults Genuinely Adult?" *The Living Light* 37, no. 1 (2000). In many ways the papers and conversations that were part of the symposium connect with points I develop further in that essay.

17. "The coordination of catechesis is not merely a strategic factor, aimed at more effective evangelization, but has a profound theological meaning. Evangelizing activity must be well coordinated because it touches on the *unity of faith*, which sustains all the Church's action" (GDC, no. 272).

3

Spirituality and Religious Education: Fostering a Closer Connection

Colleen M. Griffith

The crowded aisle in the bookstore has "spirituality" as its caption. Walking down it feels like being on safari. Exotic titles come into view and then recede alongside more traditional ones. I stop frequently along the way, sometimes out of curiosity and driven by interest, other times in sheer disbelief. How have these books come to be placed in the spirituality section? What criteria of adjudication steer the decisions of store management? How do people make their way through the spirituality maze? What guides the selection process of those who gravitate toward this corner of the bookstore?

The questions themselves command reflection. The possibility of considered response is interrupted, however, by the sound of approaching voices. A young couple turns the corner and heads down the spirituality aisle. A tall man in a baggy gray sweatshirt appears, looking uneasy. "You *like* this stuff?" he asks the cinnamon-haired woman in her late twenties beside him. "I didn't know you were so religious." She flashes a scorcher of a glance his way. "I'm not religious," she protests. "I'm spiritual."

The woman's comment is unsettling but familiar. Increased interest in spirituality in our cultural milieu has given rise to heavily traversed spirituality aisles that are approached eclectically. On the heels of this phenomenon, a most unfortunate split between spirituality and religion has crept into popular consciousness.[1]

The widening gulf between spirituality and religion is disquieting. It is attributable in part to the associations people bring to the terms *spirituality* and *religion*. Rightly or wrongly, people think positively about the word *spirituality* and less so about the word *religion*. For many, *spirituality* connotes freedom and choice, inclusivity and openness. In contrast, persons consider *religion* to be something narrow, associating it with faith institutions and with establishments thought to be stuffy and staid. The result is a magnet-like attraction to spirituality coupled, ironically, with a waning of interest in traditional religious practice. As Philip Sheldrake comments, "A widespread decline in traditional religious practice in the West runs parallel with an ever increasing hunger for spirituality."[2] Spirituality continues to gain in strength, while active participation in our churches lags.

It appears that spirituality emerges the victor here. But, in fact, the separation between spirituality and religion produces no winners. Estrangement between the two is a lose-lose situation, good for neither. A split between spirituality and religion causes spirituality to lose its rootedness in tradition and to become severed from the communal context of shared faith. And it renders religion more anemic, placing religious institutions on the defensive, leading to some desperate attempts on the part of institutional leadership to control people's beliefs and practices.

There are enough signs to suggest that these are real rather than imagined dangers. We've seen the impoverishment of spiritualities that have regressed to privatistic endeavors. We've experienced the exclusivity, legalism, and clericalism of religious institutions that have led with clutched fists rather than open palms of welcome, compassion, and equality.

Sandra Schneiders describes three contemporary ways of construing the relationship between spirituality and religion.[3] A first possibility is to consider the two as strangers, disconnected from one another in every respect. A second option is to regard them as separate but related realities, recognizing that they sometimes stand in conflict with one another. Still a third way of viewing the relationship between spirituality and religion is to see and affirm a valuable partnership between the two. This is the option favored by Schneiders, and she argues persuasively for it.

Opposed to a "disaffiliated" spirituality, which is severed from community having once known it, or an "unaffiliated" spirituality, which is deprived of the riches of any organic religious tradition, Schneiders concludes that "religion is the optional context for spirituality. The great religious traditions of the world are much more adequate matrices for spiritual development and practice than personally constructed amalgams of beliefs and practices."[4] Having claimed this, she is quick to admit the shortcomings and sinfulness of religion in its institutionalized forms. She states that it can require "an uncommon faith and integrity" to find resources for deepening one's spirituality from one's participation in the life of an institution, given that institutions are often poor representatives of tradition.[5]

The mutuality reflected in the model of partnership proposed by Schneiders stands as a powerful corrective to the separation of spirituality and religion. For partnership to become a more perceivable reality, however, there must be intentional fostering of the connection between spirituality and religion in pastoral praxis. One primary place in which the link between the two can be nurtured and explored is in religious education/catechesis.[6] It is here that persons gain access to the Christian tradition and its ways of lived faith. The comprehensive vision of total catechesis, suggested by Thomas

Groome, becomes more imaginable and efficacious when spirituality and religious education are brought closer together.[7]

Spirituality and Catechetical Education

Do people sense an intrinsic connection between "religion" and "spirituality" as a result of their experiences of catechetical education? A reading of the "signs of the times" suggests that this is not always so. To foster closer connection between religion and spirituality, religious educators need to focus more explicitly on the nature of catechetical education with respect to spirituality. What *is* the relationship between spirituality and education in faith?

Some may be tempted to dismiss this question prematurely, arguing that the connection between spirituality and catechetical education is an obvious one of symbiosis that has always been. I claim that connection between the two has been implied and assumed rather than explicitly delineated and intentionally considered. I suspect that religious educators/catechists themselves have very different senses of how spirituality and catechetical education are related, and that these differences in perception shape actual practice.[8]

How do you, the reader, construe the relationship between these two? Consider the following set of diagrams and choose the one that best portrays what you sense to be the most adequate relationship between spirituality and catechetical education:

How does your understanding of the relationship between these two shape your catechetical practice?

Diagram 1 presents catechetical education as a large enterprise that has some elements in common with spirituality. Diagram 2 depicts spirituality as the wider reality, one that overlaps catechetical education but has separate dimensions as well. Diagram 3 sets catechetical education within the larger expanse of spirituality. Diagram 4 portrays the two as separate entities with limited points of tangency,

_____ Catechetical Education
. . . . Spirituality

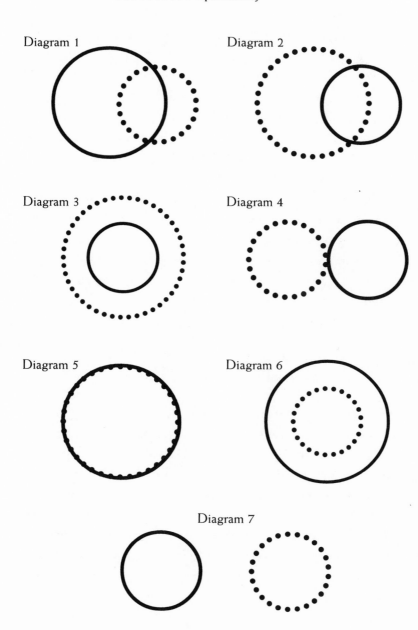

entities that appear as one and the same in Diagram 5. Spirituality gets placed in the larger ambit of catechetical education in Diagram 6, while Diagram 7 shows the two as separate enterprises.

I wish to make a strong case for Diagram 3, for catechetical education being held within the larger ambit of a Christian spirituality.[9] In using the term *Christian spirituality* I am referring to a consciously lived relationship with God in Christ, through the indwelling of the Spirit, in the context of a Christian community of faith in midst of the world.[10] I regard all of the practices that sustain and deepen a consciously lived relationship with God in Christ to be part and parcel of a Christian spirituality.

Setting catechetical education in the larger expanse of a Christian spirituality is an enormously rich way of construing the relationship between the two for at least three reasons: (1) it leads to a more holistic understanding of the *nature* of catechetical practice itself; (2) it offers an enhanced sense of the *purpose* of catechetical education; and (3) it focuses attention on the spirituality of the teaching self, the *who* that educates. Let us consider each in turn.

A Wholesome Understanding of the Nature of Catechetical Activity

Proponents of a dual understanding of religious education/catechesis maintain that there are two "moments" in catechetical practice. One involves an imparting of knowledge *about* Christian faith, and the other a nurturing *in* the ways of Christian faith. The distinctiveness of each receives emphasis in potentially dualistic terms from Gayle Felton, who writes, "The goals of Christian teaching must always include both the enhancement of cognitive knowledge and the encouragement of conversion and personal commitment."[11] On the one hand, participants in a teaching/learning event must gain access to the core Christian beliefs and symbols that can inform them. On the other, they also must enter into the kinds of experiences of Christian prayer, prophetic witness, and service that can form them. Catechetical education, alas, emerges double faced, its nature twofold.

If the dance of catechetical practice gets presented as a two step, with the moves of "formation" and "information" being those to which one should attend, connection between the two becomes lost. One forgets too quickly that information about Christian faith is ever for the sake of deeper living, and that formation in faith is precisely what inspires new levels of knowing. This dual understanding of the nature of catechetical activity is less than whole; it falls short of the holistic vision of what the *General Directory for Catechesis* (GDC) calls "an integral Christian education" (no. 122).

As catechetical education gets situated squarely in the larger context of Christian spirituality (Diagram 3), it becomes more difficult to separate information about faith and formation in faith. When catechetical educators view the goal of catechetical activity to be a rich and lively Christian spirituality for life, then teaching *what* Christians hold to be true and teaching *how* Christians practice that truth become inextricably bound. Knowledge of the facts of the Christian story remains essential, *specifically because that knowledge forms Christian identity, inviting more loving, just, and hopeful living.* Engagement in the practices of the Christian community continues to be central, *precisely because such participation offers fuller knowledge of faith.* Catechetical education that is set within the larger ambit of Christian spirituality seeks to appropriate a comprehensive, transformative vision that holds together specific ways of thinking as a Christian (beliefs) and being one (practice).

There are those who will oppose the grounding of catechetical education in spirituality, convinced that Christian religious education should be a presentation of the objective truths of faith. But what exactly is meant by "objective truth" in the first place, and does such "truth" ever exist for its own sake alone? Knowledge of the propositions of faith is not enough. Thomas Groome explains: "Beyond knowing about God, we want people to consciously live their lives in relationship with God; beyond knowing about Jesus, we want them to become disciples; beyond knowing about justice, we want them to become just, and so on."[12] A concern for the content of Christian faith is forever well advised, but it is insufficient unto itself. Fullness of Christian life requires embracing one's spiritual potential, integrating one's heart and intellect in a stance of lived faith, and being committed to embodying gospel values in the world.

An Enhanced Sense of Purpose

As catechetical education gets situated within the larger ambit of spirituality, educating for *spiritual maturity* becomes a primary goal. The biblical tradition reveals spiritual maturity as the fruit of relational life with God, something that manifests itself in deep and inclusive love that is both compassionate and just. To identify spiritual maturity as the purpose of catechetical activity is to make relational life with God, and love for humanity and the world one's primary focus.[13]

Joann Wolski Conn suggests that to ask the question, "How can we become spiritually mature?" is, by implication, to ask, "How can we realize our spiritual potential?"[14] Catechists who seek to enable others to recognize their spiritual potential already educate for spiritual maturity. Yet there are ways to be more intentional about this. Conn claims that spiritual maturity requires a practice of discernment, a way of contemplation, and the kind of self-knowledge that makes authenticity possible.[15] These core elements provide a rich springboard for reflection.

If the practice of discernment is central in coming to spiritual maturity, then one's pedagogical approach as a catechetical educator should allow for careful discernment of the full subject matter being taught[16] and built-in room for discernment of one's lived response.[17] If spiritual maturity requires a habit of contemplation enabling one to become what it is he or she beholds, then the teaching/learning event should include time for gazing, for beholding whatever element of the Christian story has come into view so that it can be appropriated more fully. Finally, if self-knowledge is a constitutive dimension of spiritual maturity, then inviting participants in a teaching/learning event to pause before their own experience, to reflect on it, to pay attention to movements within, and to notice the decisions that are emerging becomes a key role of the catechetical leader.

Catechetical practice that intentionally incorporates explicit practices of discernment and contemplation and fosters self-awareness for the sake of greater authenticity, will be education for "wide-awakeness" with respect to the activity of God in people's lives. While posing challenges to traditional pedagogical styles, this way of educating toward spiritual maturity provides fresh accents for thinking about catechetical education as "a school of faith," "an apprenticeship in Christian life" (GDC, no. 30).

The Spirituality of the Educator

Setting catechetical education in the larger expanse of a Christian spirituality focuses fresh attention on the spirituality of the teaching self. Some claim that this is an intangible variable, but, in fact, nothing is more "visible" or central to educating in faith. What matters in catechetical activity has everything to do with the heart of the educator. Good textbooks can influence people, as can sound curricula and creative pedagogical approaches. But persons are changed profoundly by educators who care about, challenge, affirm, and love them.

The spirituality of the catechetical educator makes itself manifest in live passion for the subjects of the teaching/learning enterprise, in empathy with the life experiences and struggles of others, sensitivity to persons' readiness and contexts, and a fundamental desire that co-learners have the opportunity to deepen their recognition of God, others, and the world. These are qualities of selfhood developed over time, requiring cultivation and renewal.

What is "the inner landscape of the teaching self"? Parker Palmer asks.[18] The question provides an incisive point of entry for revelation and renewal. What is the place from which I teach? Is it one of fear, obligation, curiosity, honesty, or compassion? What is the heart I long for in this ministerial activity?

The "inner landscape of the teaching self" gets buffeted about often in catechetical practice. Teaching proves to be a repeated exercise in vulnerability. The challenges of live encounter abound in catechetical moments. And there is always the likelihood of failing, of bumbling, of being less than true, regardless of one's number of years in catechetical leadership. One can speak readily about the human experience of poverty of spirit if one has been a catechetical educator.

Becoming more reflective about our own inner landscapes serves to improve the quality of our teaching. As we turn homeward toward center, we regain a sense of connection to a larger Mystery and know well our desire for God. We return to the subject matter at hand with reverence, becoming teachable once again ourselves.

Without a spirituality to sustain us, we quickly lose our sense of vocation. Mark Schwehn writes: "Absent faith, our calling will become an intolerable and lonely burden. Absent a deep commitment to the truth and a deeper conviction of it, our vocation will diminish to mere career."[19] There is a caution here that can benefit catechist formation work. The GDC notes that "the adequate formation of catechists cannot be overlooked by concerns such as the updating of texts and the reorganization of catechesis" (no. 234). Formation that doesn't provide access to the tools and practices that can deepen a catechist's own spirituality is inadequate formation. The question *"Who* am I that educates?" is as significant as the questions *"What* will I teach?" and *"How* will I teach it?" There are numerous ways in which it is more significant.

The future of catechetical education clearly requires a closer relationship between spirituality and catechesis/religious education. However one construes these two, the "signs of the times" urge more explicit linkage between them. There are many ways of establishing this link. Setting catechetical education in the larger context of Christian spirituality is one that provides a more holistic understanding of the nature of catechetical activity, offers a rich sense of purpose, and highlights the importance of the spirituality of the educator in faith.

As Christian religious educators catch sight of the possibilities inherent in an understanding of catechetical activity set in the larger ambit of a Christian spirituality, fresh points of emphasis will emerge for pedagogical practice. In addition, catechetical education will be contributing to a narrowing of the now widening gap between *spirituality* and *religion* so evident in our cultural milieu, a gap that has already diminished both. Any way one looks at it, that is a win-win scenario for us all.

Notes

1. Harold Horell describes the split between spirituality and religion as "a common postmodern refrain." He considers some of the problems associated with a spirituality disconnected from a faith community in his essay in this collection.
2. Philip Sheldrake S.J., *Spirituality and Theology: Christian Living and the Doctrine of God* (Maryknoll, N.Y.: Orbis Books, 1998), 5.
3. See Sandra M. Schneiders, I.H.M., "Religion and Spirituality: Strangers, Rivals, or Partners?" *Santa Clara Lectures* 6, no. 2 (2000): 1–26.
4. Ibid., 13.
5. Ibid., 11.
6. Debate over use of *catechesis or religious education* continues. I understand these to be integral dimensions of the same whole and therefore tend to use the terms interchangeably. In an effort to accent the necessity of both socialization/formation and education in faith, I have opted to adopt the term *catechetical education* for the practice of educating/forming in faith. This is a term suggested by Thomas Groome in his essay in this collection. It signals an attempt to hold together all that "informs, forms, and transforms" our catechetical practices.
7. For a definition of *total catechesis,* see Groome's essay herein.

8. At the national symposium entitled "The Future of Religious Education" held at Boston College in the summer of 2000, responses to the question regarding the relationship between spirituality and religious education were markedly varied and diverse.

9. Here I am referring specifically to *Christian* religious education. However, when religious education is more broadly construed, setting it in the context of a spirituality remains imperative.

10. This definition echoes the description of spirituality offered by Philip Sheldrake. See Sheldrake, *Spirituality and Theology: Christian Living and the Doctrine of God* (Maryknoll, NY: Orbis Books, 1999), 35.

11. Gayle Felton, "John Wesley and the Teaching of Ministry: Ramifications for Education in the Church Today," *Religious Education* 92, no. 1 (Winter 1997), 104.

12. Thomas H. Groome, "Spirituality as Purpose and Process of Catechesis," in *The Echo Within*, ed. Catherine Dooley and Mary Collins (Allen, Tex.: Thomas More, 1997), 161.

13. In assuming spiritual maturity to be the goal, one recognizes that education in faith is a lifelong process. The necessity of continued formation underscores the importance of adult education. For extensive treatment of the kind of adult faith formation that has the potential to transform institutions, see Jane Regan's essay in this collection.

14. Joann Wolski Conn, "Toward Spiritual Maturity," in *Freeing Theology: The Essentials of Theology in Feminist Perspective*, ed. Catherine Mowry LaCugna (San Francisco: HarperSanFrancisco, 1993), 240.

15. Ibid., 240.

16. Educating for spiritual maturity means providing access to the full tradition—its wisdom, insights, distortions, and shortsightedness.

17. Tom Beaudoin highlights the importance of people receiving tools for discernment and emphasizes the need for "clear and authentic *examples* of discernment, and teachers who can be *exemplars* of discernment, mentors who will risk sharing their struggles to live an adult Christian life" (see Tom Beaudoin's essay in this collection).

18. Parker J. Palmer, *The Courage to Teach* (San Francisco: Jossey-Bass, 1998), 4.

19. Mark Schwehn, "The Spirit of Teaching," *Conversations: On Jesuit Higher Education* 10 (Fall 1996), 15.

4

"Virtual" Catechesis: Religious Formation of the Post–Vatican II Generations

Tom Beaudoin

Although it was published in 1979, *On Catechesis in Our Time* features a challenge to catechesis and religious education that is only now beginning to be fully recognized in the Catholic Church in the United States. "Catechetical works," John Paul II exhorts, "must be linked with the real life of the generation to which they are addressed, showing close acquaintance with its anxieties and questionings, struggles and hopes." It follows that catechesis should be conducted in "a language comprehensible to the generation in question."[1] Responding vibrantly to these challenges is one of the most important tasks for catechesis and religious education in our day, for we are now confronted by the reality of three distinct generational layers within Catholicism: the generations who came of age before Vatican II, during the Vatican II era, and after Vatican II. Attending more carefully to what joins and separates these generations is one essential component in building the sort of integrated education in faith of which Thomas Groome has written.[2]

A Church of Generations

Within the Catholic Church a mass of reflection on generational differences is emerging from pastoral ministry and theology.[3]
The church yet stands in need of further practical-theological reflection and research from the standpoint of specific and diverse cultures,
classes, and genders. In addition to this work, official church documents also recognize the existence of different generations within the
contemporary church. For example, the 1996 U.S. bishops' pastoral
plan for young adult ministry, *Sons and Daughters of the Light*, refers to
important shifts in Catholic identity across generations. One important touchstone in church teaching that warrants this new interest in
generations is the Second Vatican Council's discussion of the "sense
of faith" of the "people of God." As elaborated by Karl Rahner, we
may not understand this "people of God" as one homogeneous mass,
whose "sense of faith" takes place in some ideal place. Instead, the
people of God is a collection of many *peoples*, each with different
experiences, histories, and cultures. The identities of these peoples
can legitimately be studied by social-scientific and other cultural and
anthropological methods.[4]

For catechesis and religious education, the implications of these
developments for the "real life" of Catholic generations are profound.
Once an awareness of generational differences captures the imaginations of ministers, educators, and theologians, catechesis and religious education can and must gain an irreversibly generational
valence. We may see, as if for the first time, the ways in which every
event of religious formation or instruction is an exercise in generational "politics," whether of generational peers or inter-generational
interlocutors.

This realization dovetails with the insight, growing over the
past several decades, that every event of religious education is always
also a *cultural* event—at best, an exercise in dialogue between people
of different cultures. The "inculturation" of the gospel and the gener-

ational incarnation of the gospel are two sides of the same coin.[5] Both allow that the gospel continually finds genuinely *new* expression—in diverse cultures and generations—on the one hand; and both provide genuinely new resources to better understand the gospel *itself*, on the other. So, for example, inculturation turns us not only to the question of how the gospel is "translated" into different cultures today, but how concepts, practices, and assumptions of various cultures contributed to the articulation of the gospel itself in the New Testament and early Christianity. A similar claim can be made for generational consciousness. It turns us not only to the important problems of finding language comprehensible to the generation in question, but to investigating how different generations within the New Testament period and early Christianity made use of the gospel according to their varying concerns. Of course, as is true of the concept of *culture*, one need not necessarily assume that the concept of a *generation* may simplistically be read back into early Christianity in the way that we employ the word *generation* today.

As suggested earlier, the primary differences about Catholic identity among generations in the church today are grounded in differing relationships to the Second Vatican Council (1962–65). The council functions as a fundamental reference point with respect to which different assumptions about Catholic life can be charted. Much depends on whether one was shaped most significantly by pre-council Catholicism, by the revolution introduced by the council, or by the decades since the council's conclusion. It could fairly be said that each generational layer grew into faith in relationship to quite different "signs of the times"—in the culture and in the church—within each era.

What is basically at stake in the differences among these three groups is Catholic identity itself. Catholic identity, while retaining some core characteristics across generations, quite naturally takes somewhat different forms as it is incarnated in different eras. Thus, the three main groups in the church today each understand what it means to be Catholic in a somewhat different way: whether in approach to official church teachings in general, attitudes about particular teachings, personal piety, social justice, evangelization, Mary, other religions, or sexuality. This is not to ignore, of course, what Catholics tend to share about Catholic identity across generations. For example, Andrew Greeley argues that Catholics more or less share a unique "sacramental imagination."[6]

"Virtual" and "Real" Catechesis: The Background

I begin this section with a widely observed fact: To a very deep degree, the religious formation and education of young generations—what the *General Directory for Catechesis* (GDC) calls their "formative journey" (no. 145)—takes place as much, or more, in the secular culture as in explicitly religious spaces. This phenomenon is one important aspect of postmodern culture. This fact of young adult life is recognized by the GDC when it observes that "younger generations…are the users and creative subjects of mass media communications" (no. 162). I name this reality "virtual" catechesis, a reality that is genuinely new in its depth and intensity for the Catholic Church in societies undergoing secularization. Rather than simply setting up an opposition between the church's truth or teaching and that of the culture, attending to the reality of "virtual" catechesis offers a more adequate construal of the relationship between catechesis and culture in North American and other societies.

One of the chief insights of twentieth-century sociology, anthropology, and theology is that religious meaning is always negotiated with respect to the mental "furniture" borrowed from one's cultural environment and in connection with the immediate politics of value at play in one's social world. Such values can and do arise from, and are reinforced by, somewhat "invisible" forces, such as socioeconomic structures and family histories. Part of the new reality, however, is that they also arise from and are reinforced by more concrete and daily experiences within popular media culture, such as movies, sporting events, music, television, and the Internet. I have found, for example, that there are few young adults who cannot identify a meaningful or spiritual moment, scene, song, or experience from their popular media culture; they carry this moment with them as part of their spiritual autobiography and as a spiritual tool for making sense of their life experiences. These popular media culture aspects of daily life provide important elements of the milieu in which God's grace is appropriated, religious meaning is negotiated, and political work is undertaken.

If we may accurately schematize such "virtual" catechesis, then we must also unpack "real" catechesis. By "real" catechesis I mean intentional religious formation and education self-consciously associated with and sponsored by representatives of the Christian tradition. In making this distinction the terms *virtual* and *real* must be kept in quotation marks to signify that, in practice, both forms of catechesis influence the religious identity of believers, making them work out their salvation with the materials of these two catecheses. Moreover, this distinction is always something of a ruse; these two catecheses themselves mutually influence each other and use each other's materials both intentionally and unintentionally.[7] Obviously very unlike the popular cultures of the early church, much of the popular cultures of young adults today is governed by the electronic media. The GDC is perhaps more correct than its authors realize in claiming that the "media [have] become essential for evangelization and catechesis" (no. 160)—both "virtual" and "real."

Several documents from recent ecclesial teaching provide resources for recognizing and theologizing about the existence of such a "virtual" catechesis. This may be the case even if the documents themselves do not explicitly or consistently endorse such a concept.

First, the importance of the use of natural signs in catechesis opens us to consider "virtual" catechesis. The *National Catechetical Directory* (NCD) describes catechesis as having one source which is given in four signs. This singular source is "God's word, fully revealed in Jesus Christ and at work in the lives of people exercising their faith under the guidance of the Magisterium, which alone teaches authentically."[8] The four signs are biblical, liturgical, ecclesial, and natural. The natural sign includes "examining at the most profound level the meaning and value of everything created, *including the products of human effort*, in order to show how all creation sheds light on the mystery of God's saving power and is in turn illuminated by it" (NCD, no. 46, emphasis added). This teaching creates an opening for both the experience of the natural world and of human popular cultures to be construed as a sign of, or a gateway to, the source of catechesis.[9]

Second, alongside the "great professions of faith of the Magisterium," official documents on catechesis have also endorsed "popular professions of faith," such as popular songs.[10] The fact that they arise out of "the traditional Christian culture of certain countries" need not necessarily imply that the popular cultures of more secularized countries could not also produce artistic products that gain the status of a faith profession among youth, insofar as human values consistent with Christian values may yet be found in even the most thoroughly "secularized" cultures.[11]

Third, by employing the category of "quasi-catechumens," church documents seem to acknowledge a state of possessing Christian formation that is neither complete and formal nor fundamentally distorted, lacking in formal religious knowledge but not necessarily lacking in spiritual experience.[12] Those schooled in largely "virtual" catechesis might in fact fit this state.

Fourth, official teaching recognizes a need for catechesis to take into itself "signs of the times" in its own context, signs that may indeed bear seeds of the word. The GDC recognizes that faith "must be rooted in human experience and not remain a mere adjunct to the human person" (no. 87). That human experience may indeed bear seeds of the word through "genuine religious and moral values...sown in human society and diverse cultures" (no. 95; see also nos. 200, 203–4). That such genuine religious and moral values could and must be present in the various practices of popular culture would seem to be a corollary of such a conviction.

Fifth and finally, another point of entry for the introduction of this realm of "virtual" catechesis is the central role of inculturation in catechesis. The GDC claims that "in the light of the Gospel, the Church must appropriate all the positive values of culture and of cultures and reject those elements which impede development of the true potential of persons and peoples" (no. 21; see also nos. 109–10). In agreement, the adult ministry pastoral plan *Our Hearts Were Burning Within Us* creates the space for this exchange when it asserts that "inculturation is a process of mutual enrichment between the gospel and culture"[13]—or in the present terms, a mutual enrichment between "real" and "virtual" catechesis. A Christian optimism makes it possible to discern within cultures themselves, in the strong formulation of the GDC, "what has an authentic Gospel value" (no. 204).

Taking these cues from church documents, as well as the measure of these signs of the times, one irreplaceable goal of catechesis and religious education with young adults must be correlating "virtual" catechesis with "real" catechesis toward a catechetical experience that helps young adults "to perceive the action of God throughout the formative journey" (no. 145). "Virtual" catechesis does and should exercise a relative and "legitimate" autonomy from formal church structures, insofar as it reflects the uniqueness of the charisms and apostolate proper to the people of God, especially the laity, in the secular sphere.

"Virtual" and "Real" Catechesis: Similarities and Differences

Some differences and similarities between "virtual" and "real" catechesis, as practiced, may be distinguished. Whereas "virtual" catechesis is typically present over the course of childhood, adolescence,

and young adulthood, indeed throughout one's entire life, "real" catechesis is now frequently absent or merely occasional—particularly in
the lives of young adults. Further, "virtual" catechesis tends to be *fragmentary*, a form of religious education in disparate parts that makes no
claim to a unified whole or holistic vision of life. In other words, "virtual" catechesis educates in values or visions of life that are not
anchored in a single central vision or way of life. "Real" catechesis, by
contrast, tends to be *fragmented*, or a form of religious education, in disparate parts, of a nonsystematically presented whole. In other words,
because it is so rare in the life of the young adult, "real" catechesis—
when it occurs—often offers nothing more than small pieces of a whole
vision of Christian life, like misshapen chips from a shattered vase.[14]

Further differences can be elaborated. Ecclesial affiliation is typically entirely optional for the experience of "virtual" catechesis,
whereas it is usually present during "real" catechesis. This difference
is related to "virtual" catechesis being unaccountable, on its own
terms, to a particular concrete tradition. By contrast, "real" catechesis,
on its own terms, is absolutely accountable to Catholic tradition.[15]
Moreover, whereas the former renders most young adults quite liter-
ate (for example, in different forms of popular culture), the latter typically has rendered contemporary young adults semiliterate in
Catholic religious concepts and practices.

There are some commonalities between the two catecheses.
"Virtual" catechesis and "real" catechesis both function to help
people "make do" with their lives, while at the same time they have
both often attempted to control the lives of those same people
through subtle exercises. A history of grace and its opposite may be
found in both. They both potentially offer a "communication of the
faith [that is] an event of grace, realized in the encounter of the word
of God with the experience of the person. It is expressed in sensible
signs and is ultimately open to mystery." Both "virtual" and "real" catechesis "can happen in diverse ways, not always completely known
to us" (no. 150).

In sum, if catechists will attend to "virtual" catechesis, they will be more likely to allow "real" catechesis its fullest expression, as a "pedagogy of the incarnation" (no. 143). Correlating "virtual" and "real" catechesis renders practicable the profound assertion in the GDC that "experience, assumed by faith, becomes in a certain manner, a locus for the manifestation and realization of salvation, where God, consistently with the pedagogy of the Incarnation, reaches man with his grace and saves him" (no. 152). Correlating "virtual" and "real" catechesis, which is also a "correlation and interaction between profound human experiences and the revealed message" (no. 153) or "correlating the various aspects of the Christian message with the concrete life of man" (no. 241) will free the catechist to "teach the person to read his own lived experience in this regard" (no. 152). This correlation may even lead to "new expressions of the Gospel in the culture in which it has been planted," including the various cultures in which young adults live today, which the catechist is charged to help "stimulate" (no. 208).

Ways Forward: A Proposal

How would this correlation of "virtual" and "real" catechesis appear were it broken into specific tasks for catechesis and religious education for young adults? I offer the following as foundation stones in formulating approaches for religious education of the post–Vatican II generations, based on a correlation of Catholic analysis of younger generations with my experiences in ministry with young adults.

- *Uniting religion and spirituality, where these have become sundered in the lives of young adults.* Ways must be provided of linking the interior and experiential to the exterior, conceptual and doctrinal. This requires dignifying the authenticity of the spirituality already practiced by young adults, with the catechist or religious educator careful to affirm what can be affirmed and sensitive to the unofficial and subjugated knowledge in which the spirituality of young people is often expressed. Further, teachers may well consider the spiritualities that inform the doctrine or concept that they would like to teach young adults and develop exercises and practices that invite them into such spiritualities. For example, teaching about the Trinity—God *as* family—is an invitation to connect this doctrine to the spiritual practices of authentic family.[16] As we steward the yoking of religion and spirituality, we must keep in mind the church's convictions about the importance of a searching faith that questions, probes, critically reflects, and even doubts.[17]

• *Uniting spirituality and politics.* One implication here is to build religious curriculum out of service projects that attract the self-sacrificing impulses of many young people. These experiences may then be drawn out further by engagement with scripture and tradition vis-à-vis political work, toward a more holistic political identity. For example, I worked with one group of young adults at a soup kitchen, after which we debriefed our experience by making a list of certain values about which their service experience convinced them more deeply. In later meetings we opened the scriptures and tradition in order to nuance and elaborate those values. That was followed by generalizing those values to difficult moral issues, such as the death penalty and abortion. The purpose was to allow core gospel values to be claimed by young adults themselves, from their experience, that could then be generalized across significant moral issues, for the sake of uniting spirituality and politics more consciously.

• *Fostering religious literacy.* Such an urgent task must not become simply a return to the catechism but a fostering of the "catechism of head and heart," so that there is no literacy about any part of the Christian symbolic world apart from a specific practice, an existential significance for the young adult.[18] Among formally educated young adults we may take up reasonable portions of classic or forgotten Christian texts—not just contemporary spiritual books—in small reading circles or book clubs. So, for example, by reading together a chapter of Augustine's *Confessions* with a competent discussion leader, young adults may both gain literacy in a classical work from the Christian tradition that, once they enter into Augustine's struggles, does not seem so foreign as they perhaps supposed, and discover a new way of discerning sin and grace in their own daily lives, inspired by Augustine. In communities with less formal education we may still make literacy a regular rhythm in pedagogical events, for example, by giving access to a diversity of prayer and musical practices from the tradition, regularly naming Catholic values and practices *as* Catholic, and featuring both ancient and contemporary Christian symbols and language during liturgy. In all settings literacy will be fostered if we take care that the fundamental elements of Catholic identity—and their everyday practice—are regularly highlighted. If some sense of the breadth and depth of the church's tradition is not experienced as the "communication of the living mystery of God"[19] this tradition-become-traditionalism may rightly be rejected by many young adults.

• *Teaching our tradition as a toolbox for discerning sin and grace in popular media culture in particular and everyday life in general.* This will require prioritizing formation in the spiritual skill of discernment. Whether the discernment model to be appropriated in particular situations is from Ignatius, or from medieval women theologians, or from elsewhere, it is imperative that we sponsor young adults in taking up a relationship to their own concrete history of sin and grace.[20] This includes sin and grace in their own unique experiences of "virtual" catechesis. Indispensable will be catechetical development of reliable Catholic *patterns* of discernment, clear and authentic *examples* of discernment, and teachers who can be *exemplars* of discernment, mentors who will risk sharing their struggles to live an adult Christian life. Success in teaching our tradition in this manner may well be measured in fundamental ways: the degree to which young adults develop a "critical maturity" in approaching media culture (GDC, no 209), and a heightened "passion for the truth," as well as a deepened praxis of the "defense of liberty," "respect for the dignity of individuals," and an "elevation of the authentic culture of peoples" (GDC, no. 162).

• *Helping young adults foster a rightly formed conscience.* This is "one of the most important aspects in ministry today."[21] Confronted by a seemingly ever-expanding world of religious, philosophical, sexual, and ethnic pluralism, and by a church that is occasionally tempted to declaim magisterial teaching as if by fiat, practical helps to young adults in making their way morally through this world are often welcomed or at least considered if they are presented as an invitation, without relying on overly religious jargon and without an attempt to coerce the young adults into a larger religious or political program. Catholicism bears a strong tradition of the centrality of conscience, and working step by step with young adults in formation of conscience on difficult issues will be one essential element in encouraging younger generations to embrace freely and maturely the truths of the Catholic tradition.

• *Encouraging a balance of engagement with the world and withdrawal from it.* Living in a world in which there is constant pressure for persons or things to be productive, catechesis and religious education may offer young adults the profound gift of

a pedagogy of encounter with silence. For example, I typically schedule an extended period of silence during young
adult retreats, and this silence often provokes at least a mild
crisis, in the positive sense, of allowing attendance to
thoughts and hungers and sensations that young adults' busy
lives may have suppressed or deflected. Working with young
adults' responses to extended silence in a useful way, perhaps
through various discernment exercises, will be a challenging
element of this pedagogy. However difficult this may prove,
many of the great spiritual writers of our tradition have
known that the silence that leads to true interiority and real
self-confrontation is a singular precondition for genuine spiritual growth.

- *Sponsoring spiritual mentoring.* Young adults frequently desire spiritual mentors, trusted adults who represent fidelity to a mature
Christian life. Spiritual mentoring can take many religious-
educational forms, from fostering inter-generational relationships to formal spiritual direction. As an example of the
former, I worked with one young adult ministry to organize an
evening of conversation on the challenges to being family
today. Church members from all generations were invited to
participate. The evening began with the young adults talking
about their experiences of their families in the 1980s. Middle-
aged adults then shared how difficult it was to parent a family
in the 1970s and 1980s, how unprepared they were for the
changes in lifestyles and values of their children, and what it
was like to return from service in Vietnam and reintegrate into
the family. Older generations shared their stories of the meaning of family from the Depression era and World War II. The
overall effect was that young adults received mentoring in
ways of being family from older generations. New friendships

were initiated, and new possibilities of teaching and learning were discovered in this inter-generational pedagogy.

- *Offering young families education and support.* This task is particularly crucial for a generation that has frequently gone through many potentially destabilizing family experiences. Fulfilling such a task in terms of catechesis and religious education would include regular classes on and mentoring relationships for learning parenting skills and fostering healthy relationships and providing places to explore the spiritual riches, challenges, and obligations of family life with other young parents.[22] In addition, we must explore new ways to intervene catechetically in marriage preparation, as well as in "creative followup and support for couples once they are married."[23] Religious education for children and parents must be more tightly linked than ever, so that the "virtual" catechesis of the world affecting the home will be more likely to engage explicitly the "real" catechesis sponsored by the church.

- *Helping relate spiritual growth and psychological maturing.* Because we are redeemed as whole persons, growth in faith always has implications for the whole person. Catechists and religious educators, even working in tandem with spiritual directors, can provide clues about the relationship between mental health and spiritual maturity, the "integral development of the human person and of all peoples" (GDC, no. 18), "developing a holistic and healthy understanding of life [while] deepening one's relationship to God."[24] It is instructive that the U.S. bishops' document on young adult ministry encourages such holistic formation: "evangelization, catechesis, and pastoral care."[25] Much of the "virtual" catechesis in which young adults engage will already be couched in popular psychological language.[26] Concern for psychological well-being on the part of young adults is an opportunity for religious education that need not only result in the "reduction" of the gospel to psychologistic language.

- *Revitalizing the religious imagination.* Young adults bring imaginations already deeply marked by experiences in various popular ethnic and media cultures. Oftentimes these imaginations are prepared to take more risks in relating to God and in imaging their spiritual development than those who represent "real" catechesis are willing to allow. Catherine Lacugna rightly observes that with respect to Christians' image of the Trinity, "there is no doubt that the heavy masculine imagery for God has deadened the Christian imagination."[27] And Juan Luis Segundo underscores the social implications of a passive religious imagination: "By deforming God we protect our own egotism. Our falsified and inauthentic ways of dealing with our fellow men are allied to our falsification of the idea of God. Our unjust society and our perverted idea of God are in close and terrible alliance."[28] Catechesis and religious education will need to resource the imaginations of young adults with respect to their images of God, Jesus, and their own spiritual development, and help young adults critically interrelate those imaginations with the tradition's rich storehouse of religious imagination. This will likely require catechesis and religious education to broaden their approaches beyond didactic and verbal/conceptual ways of knowing, to take seriously the resources for imagination present in the art and media of both "virtual" and "real" catechesis. Even John Paul II made some initial steps in this direction by engaging the music of Bob Dylan in a humorous and memorable engagement of "virtual" and "real" catechesis.[29]

If catechists can steward young adults in relating "virtual" and "real" catechesis, they will find themselves on the leading edge of ministry in the coming century. They will have much to teach theologians, liturgists, and all ministers who work for a future church that is both genuinely new and authentically Catholic.

Notes

1. John Paul II, *On Catechesis in Our Time* (Washington, D.C.: United States Catholic Conference, 1979), no. 49.
2. See Groome's essay in this collection.
3. Among book-length works are Robert Ludwig, *Reconstructing Catholicism for a New Generation* (New York: Crossroad, 1995); James Davidson, *The Search for Common Ground: What Unites and Divides Catholic Americans* (Huntington, Ind.: Our Sunday Visitor, 1997); and Dean Hoge et al., *Young Adult Catholics: Religion in the Culture of Choice* (Notre Dame, Ind.: University of Notre Dame Press, 2001).
4. See *Lumen Gentium*, in *Vatican Council II: Volume 1: The Conciliar and Postconciliar Documents*, ed. Austin Flannery (Northport, N.Y.: Costello Publishing Co., 1996), 363–64, no. 12. Relevant passages include: "The holy People of God shares also in Christ's prophetic office....The whole body of the faithful who have an anointing that comes from the holy one...cannot err in matters of belief. This characteristic is shown in the supernatural appreciation of the faith of the whole people, when 'from the bishops to the last of the faithful' they manifest a universal consent in matters of faith and morals....The people unfailingly adheres to this faith, penetrates it more deeply with right judgment, and applies it more fully in daily life." See also Karl Rahner, "The Relation Between Theology and Popular Religion," trans. Joseph Donceel, in *Theological Investigations* XXII (New York: Crossroad, 1991), 140–47.
5. For what I mean by *inculturation*, see Robert Schreiter, *Constructing Local Theologies* (Maryknoll, N.Y.: Orbis Books, 1985), and Aylward Shorter, *Toward a Theology of Inculturation* (Maryknoll, N.Y.: Orbis Books, 1988).
6. Andrew Greeley, *The Catholic Imagination* (Berkeley and Los Angeles: University of California Press, 2000).
7. Examples are seemingly endless of the way that "real" catechesis and church teaching reformulate, or make use of, values, practices, and problems of the local culture in which that catechesis and teaching are formulated. For one example from recent scholarship, see Bernadette Brooten, *Love Between Women: Early Christian Responses to Female Homoeroticism* (Chicago: University of Chicago Press, 1996). Brooten explores early church teaching on female homoeroticism, which reformulated popular

cultural texts and teachings (for example, from medicine and astrology) circulating in Mediterranean culture. She argues that Paul's "condemnation of sexual relations between women embodies and enforces the assumptions about gender found in nearly all the Roman-period sources on female homoeroticism" (266).

8. *Sharing the Light of Faith: National Catechetical Directory for Catholics of the United States* (Washington, D.C.: United States Catholic Conference, 1979), no. 41.

9. Catechesis should and must also engage and encourage the *production* of popular works of "virtual" catechesis by the faithful, subsequently relating them to "real" catechesis, thus stimulating the active role of the faithful in producing their own popular cultures.

10. John Paul II, *On Catechesis in Our Time*, nos. 28, 59.

11. Ibid. See also ibid., no. 54.

12. Ibid., no. 44.

13. *Our Hearts Were Burning Within Us: A Pastoral Plan for Adult Faith Formation in the United States* (Washington, D.C.: United States Catholic Conference, 1999), 28.

14. This is so despite the exhortation of the GDC that "initiatory catechesis" be "comprehensive and systematic formation" (no. 67). I am grateful to David Tracy for the distinction between *fragmented* and *fragmentary* in his 1997 lectures at Harvard Divinity School. One cannot push this distinction too far, however. It could well be argued that "virtual" catechesis, while fragmentary with respect to a coherent set of ideas or values, yet has the power to form people into the "value" of being productive consumers.

15. "Catechesis is an essentially ecclesial act" (GDC, no. 78). Again, the difference here should not be overdrawn. It could well be argued that "virtual" catechesis is accountable, though relatively invisibly, to the economic and social systems on which it depends.

16. For the systematic theological rendering of this claim, see Catherine Mowry LaCugna, *God for Us: The Trinity and Christian Life* (New York: HarperCollins, 1993). For a practical theological rendering for young adults, see Tom Beaudoin, "Three's Company," *U.S. Catholic* 65, no. 9 (September 2000): 21–24.

17. *Our Hearts Were Burning Within Us*, 17. In my view, this rich paragraph could well serve as a charter for almost all young adult ministry in the United States today.

18. Karl Rahner, *The Trinity*, trans. Joseph Donceel (New York: Crossroad, 1997), 11. Excellent in this respect are the themes and issues for catechesis

recommended in *Sons and Daughters of the Light* (Washington, D.C.: NCCB, 1996), 29.

19. John Paul II, *On Catechesis in Our Time*, no. 7.
20. The classic text is Ignatius of Loyola, *The Spiritual Exercises*, trans. Louis J. Puhl (Chicago: Loyola University Press, 1951). Widening the lens on discernment is Rosalynn Voaden, *God's Words, Women's Voices: The Discernment of Spirits in the Writing of Late-Medieval Women Visionaries* (Rochester, N.Y.: York Medieval Press, 1999).
21. *Sons and Daughters of the Light*, 36.
22. See *Our Hearts Were Burning Within Us*, 25.
23. Ray R. Noll, *Sacraments: A New Understanding for a New Generation* (Mystic, Conn.: Twenty-Third Publications, 1999), 154.
24. *Sons and Daughters of the Light*, 26.
25. Ibid.
26. "Our [non-Latino] interviewees were...likely to refer to popular spiritual gurus as diverse as M. Scott Peck, Joseph Campbell, Laura Schlesinger and James Dobson as sources from which they drew spiritual direction and support" (Dean Hoge et al, "Sources and Modes of Young Adult Catholic Spirituality," paper presented to the Society for the Scientific Study of Religion [7 November 1998], 13).
27. Lacugna, *God for Us*, 18.
28. Juan Luis Segundo, *Our Idea of God*, trans. John Drury (Maryknoll, N.Y.: Orbis Books, 1974), 8.
29. In Bologna, Italy, in 1997, "Pope John Paul II listened to Bob Dylan play some of his greatest hits and borrowed a page from the musician's songbook....'You have asked: How many roads must a man walk down before you call him a man? I answer: one. There is only one road for man, and that is Christ, who said 'I am the way,' the Pope said. Reflecting on the song's refrain, 'The answer, my friend, is blowin' in the wind,' the Pope said, 'It's true. Not, however, in the wind that blows everything away into nothingness, but in the wind that is the breath and voice of the Spirit, the voice that calls and says, 'Come'" (cited in *The Catholic Key* [Diocese of Kansas City–St. Joseph] 29, no. 32 [5 October 1997], 14).

5

Cultural Postmodernity and Christian Faith Formation

Harold Daly Horell

We are in the midst today of a broad cultural shift in the way we perceive, understand, and make sense of our lives and world. This movement is frequently referred to as a shift away from the certainty and confidence of modernity to the greater ambiguity and multiplicity of postmodernity. I explore in this essay the shift toward cultural postmodernity, examine how this shift is affecting the church, and consider the implications of the movement into postmodernity for contemporary catechesis or catechetical education.

My analysis is in accord with the vision of education in faith set forth by Thomas Groome and Jane Regan in the first two chapters of this collection. Along with Groome and Regan, and following the *General Directory for Catechesis* (GDC), I envision contemporary catechesis as a "new evangelization" or process of ongoing and lifelong education grounded in careful attention to the "signs of the times" (that is, the social, political, and existential realities of present-day life). It is aimed at providing opportunities for informing, forming, and even transforming Christians and most especially Christian congregations/parishes (as learning communities of faith) as they strive to welcome and embrace the values of God's reign ever more fully.

My focus is on cultural postmodernity and not on philosophical postmodernism. Philosophical postmodernism is an intellectual movement that has arisen within the broader cultural shift that is now taking place. It often provides systematic explorations of cultural practices and insights that arise within postmodernity. While I draw from philosophical postmodernism, I do not address postmodern philosophical quandaries directly.[1]

The Shift Toward Cultural Postmodernity

Theologians have explored ways in which ethnicity, gender, and class contribute to tensions and growing edges in the church. Additional research and reflection are required in these areas. As we look toward the future, there is another trend that theologians and pastoral ministers have only begun to address and that also deserves attention. On the surface this trend may be spoken of as a generational difference. The two most recent generations, the so-called Generation X and the Millennial Generation, have unique life experiences and, consequently, new perspectives on Christian faith.[2] At a deeper level, Generation X and the Millennial Generation are the most prominent features of a gradual yet growing cultural shift affecting people of all ages and stages of life. This shift is a movement away from modernity toward cultural postmodernity.

The essence of the cultural shift into postmodernity is captured by a story that I have taken, with a few alterations, from Walter Truett Anderson. It seems that three umpires were having a beer after a baseball game. One said, "There's balls and strikes and *I call 'em the way they are.*" The second responded, "There's balls and there's strikes and *I call 'em the way I see 'em.*" The third then remarked, "In the game of baseball I'm the umpire and there's balls and strikes, but *until I call 'em they ain't nothin.*"[3]

The first umpire's statement is characteristic of a classical worldview. From such a perspective there is an objective reality that one

82

can learn to recognize with clarity and confidence. The second umpire's remark is characteristic of a modern worldview. A modern perspective highlights the role of the person or knowing subject in relation to the broader world of which he or she is a part. The turn to the subject that marked the shift from a classical to a modern world-view is associated in Western history with the Age of Enlightenment, although in many ways Catholicism did not embrace a modern worldview until the time of the Second Vatican Council.[4]

The third umpire's response signals a movement toward a post-modern outlook. The cultural shift into postmodernity has been sparked by a growing recognition that persons and communities define or construct understandings of reality from within specific life contexts (for example, the context provided by a game of baseball) as they fill specific social roles (for example, the role of being an umpire in a game of baseball), and that without such constructions of reality there can be only ambiguity and confusion. In this case, without the umpire's determination of balls and strikes within the context of a game of baseball, there "ain't nothin.'"

Characteristics of Cultural Postmodernity

Emerging cultural postmodernity can be described more fully through an examination of six of its most common features. First, the postmodern focus on social context entails a movement away from reliance on meta-narratives (overarching and inclusive frameworks of meaning and value). Contemporary pluralism and multiculturalism, the rapid rate of change, and a growing awareness that large institu-tions often lag behind the pace of change all contribute to a sense that overarching and inclusive frameworks of meaning and value are less and less helpful in guiding our lives.[5] For some, the movement away from meta-narratives entails a rejection of such overarching frame-works. For others, overarching paradigms may remain meaningful but become secondary in importance.[6] Those opting for this latter position generally concede that even if the formulation of overarching conceptions of life and the world remains a goal, there can be no self-evident universal insights to serve as first principles of human practice and inquiry.[7]

Second, from postmodern perspectives knowledge is socially created or constructed. The play, movement, or relational network of some specific community, tradition, life situation, or, perhaps, game always provide the framework and material for developing an understanding of life and the world. Additionally, the contemporary focus on the socially constructed nature of knowledge is both an extension of modernity and, at the same time, the emergence of a new and distinct cultural outlook. On the one hand, postmodern attention to the contextual nature of knowledge builds upon the sense of historical consciousness and stress on human subjectivity that are hallmarks of modernity. On the other hand, postmodernity transforms the modern emphasis on historicity and human subjectivity. The currents of cultural postmodernity encourage us to become self-consciously (and perhaps even hyper-sensitively) aware of the ways our lives, and especially our subjective sense of ourselves, are not unified or built around a central core. Instead, from postmodern perspectives any sense of personal and social identity takes shape or is constructed within the pluriform, often ambiguous, and sometimes conflictual contexts of our lives.[8]

Overall, and this is a third defining characteristic of emerging cultural postmodernity, self and social identity are seen with increasing frequency not as givens but as projects or goals we must strive to achieve. More fully, there is growing recognition that we can no longer take for granted (if indeed we ever truly could) the existence of a unified, coherent sense of self or social identity that endures over time and serves as the center from which all thought and action emerges. Rather, postmodernity encourages us to embrace (rather than minimize) the complexities of both our various social roles and the interplay among these roles. For instance, I am a parent. In my role as a parent I am sometimes a compassionate listener, at other times a stern disciplinarian; sometimes I step in to care for my children and address their physical, emotional, and spiritual needs, while at other times I step back to encourage independence and self-sufficiency. From postmodern perspectives, I can gain a better understanding of what it means to be a parent if, rather than striving to envision parenting as unified, well-ordered life role, I recognize the multiple, complex, and conflictual dimensions of my being a parent and embrace parenting as a life project that requires ongoing reflection, adaptation, and attention to the sometimes ambiguous nature of my relationships with my sons and daughter. Moreover, I am also continually called to explore the extent to which my role as a parent can be coherently related to the roles I play as a husband, teacher, member of a Christian faith community, and in my other life projects.

Similarly, from a postmodern perspective Christian identity is never a given. Rather, if we are to avoid being self-deceptive, those of us who are Christians must always be open to asking how or in some cases whether we can make a Sunday to Monday connection. By that I mean how we might articulate, first, a sense or senses of Christian identity that come to the fore in the experience of Sunday liturgy; then, a sense or senses of social identity that address the realities of everyday family, work, and civic life that we awaken to every Monday morning; and finally explore how our senses of Christian identity might be integrated with or transform the various senses of personal and social identity that we experience in our everyday lives.[9]

Furthermore, the currents of cultural postmodernity prompt us toward greater acknowledgment of the ways our senses of self and social identity are always influenced by social pressures and internal drives of which we can never be fully aware. From postmodern perspectives, psychological theories of development and personality can be useful only if they explore how to construct successfully a multifaceted sense of identity that acknowledges the often unrecognized dynamics of social influence and inner drives and responds to the complex and sometimes ambiguous or conflictual realities of life in the twenty-first century.[10]

Fourth, the currents of postmodernity encourage a movement away from modern notions of foundational and comprehensive knowledge toward an embrace of specificity, contingency, and limitation in knowing. From a modern perspective we should strive, at least ideally, to approach most issues and concerns by beginning with first or foundational principles. For instance, to the extent that we remain within the cultural currents of modernity we are likely to respond to situations of injustice by trying to step back from the particularity of the situation, while striving to obtain as clear and complete a view of the moral issues as we possibly can. We are likely to want to formulate and then appeal to a standard of justice that is as comprehensive and universally applicable as possible.[11] In contrast, to the extent that we have been influenced by cultural postmodernity we are likely to recognize that we can never step back fully from the specificity of our personal, communal, and sociocultural standpoint. From postmodern perspectives whatever insight or wisdom we have is grounded in our past, our specific life history. Additionally, to the extent that we might have lived in another time and place or could have made different life choices, our outlook on life bears the marks of contingency. It could have been other than it is now. Similarly, postmodernity encourages us to replace seemingly universal ideals (such as modern, universalistic conceptions of justice and truth) with a more limited sense of patching together a framework for understanding life and the world from within the limited, finite outlook of a specific perspective.

The currents of cultural postmodernity encourage us to see modern effort to discover universal conceptions of justice, truth, and other ideals as illusory and false. Instead of generating universal understanding and human solidarity, the abstract reflection of modernity is more likely to produce intractable conflict as competing groups, each with its own supposedly universal ideals, confront one another. The modern focus on foundational and comprehensive knowledge can also lead to the neglect of the relationships and social bonds that are necessary for common understanding and action.[12]

In dealing with questions of meaning and value, postmodernity encourages a person to become a kind of archeologist.[13] More fully, postmodernity directs us to look toward the past to gain a realistic understanding of both present and future possibilities. From post-modern perspectives, the past is the personal and social history that is necessary for understanding how what presently exists came to be. To forget the obstacles overcome in the past could lead us to be overly optimistic. To forget the achievements of the past could deprive us of the wisdom of personal and communal experience. Hence, from postmodern perspectives, if we are to construct a sense of the meaning and value of life, we must begin by considering how core convictions have been constructed within our families, work or professional lives, faith communities, social or peer groups, and any other social spheres in which we are involved. We must explore how these central convictions have been employed, where they are in con-flict with one another, and what their potential uses and limitations are in the present. Then, we must draw from the various strands of our lives to construct a moral orientation to life. Along the way, we may forge social relationships and bonds (with family members, neighbors living down the street, or friends from around the country or world with whom we are connected by email or online/video chat technol-ogy) based on shared convictions and pledges of mutual support.

Fifth, postmodernity encourages us to question the roles played by large institutions, or at the very least to become critically reflec-tive about commitments to large institutions. Within the cultures of Western modernity, large institutions support broad frameworks of meaning and value. Churches, schools, business corporations, politi-cal parties, branches of the military, and other large institutional structures often present all-inclusive accounts of what life can and should be like. They help to shape us so that we embrace some encompassing vision of life, and they may even have ways of reprimanding us if we try to deviate from or reject what they have to offer. However, difficulties arise today because of increasing social fragmentation. To varying degrees today we may feel stretched by competing and often conflicting visions of life presented to us in our professional, social, and personal lives. As the grand visions of life presented by large institutions come to compete with one another, we may also have a sense that our own creativity and ability to be open to new possibilities are being stifled. As we become aware of the limitations of large institutions, we may come to believe that in order to pursue our life goals we need to make use of affiliations with large institutions while being careful not to let those institutions take over our lives.

A postmodern approach to institutions is illustrated by the story of Bill Gates and Microsoft. Distrusting large institutions, Gates felt he could nurture his own creative energies by working outside of established institutional structures. When his work required the creation of a public corporation, Gates created what can be called an "anti-institution institution." He assembled a work force made up almost entirely of recent college graduates whom he could form to share his emphasis on the importance of creative responses to pressing technological questions.

Many of Microsoft's "microserfs" (as they have come to be called by others in the information-technology industry) pour their energies into the projects to which they are assigned with little concern for what lies beyond their immediate charge.[14] When interviewed on National Public Radio after the Microsoft antitrust trial, a majority of the microserfs were unconcerned about the court order to break up Microsoft. Most felt that their immediate projects were what was truly important and that they would continue to do their work, whether as Microsoft employees or as the employees of some spin-off company. Expressing an outlook that is becoming more and more common as postmodernity gains ground, they regarded larger institutional frameworks as secondary, or as necessary evils. For them, the real work is done at the local not the corporate or institutional level.

Sixth, postmodernity can lead to a heightened awareness of the role of power in social life.[15] Once we realize that knowledge is socially constructed, we can recognize that those who create knowledge have social power. For instance, in the opening story umpires are shown to be powerful people in the game of baseball because they get to "call 'em balls and strikes," that is, they get to create balls and strikes by observing each pitch and classifying it. We may also recognize that those who are limited or deprived of the ability to name their world for themselves or contribute to socially constructed systems of meaning are deprived of social power. For example, in 1992, as people celebrated the so-called five-hundredth anniversary of the discovery of America, many people (including many native American groups) objected. Their objections were often based on a postmodern sense that the socially constructed notion of the *discovery* of the *previously unknown Americas* deprived our country of the history and traditions of the people who had lived on the continent for many generations before Columbus arrived.

Postmodern Attitudes

To understand postmodernity we need to recognize that uneven surfaces, rough edges, fissures, and gaps always mark the currents of culture and that emerging postmodern sensibilities give rise not to one but to a range of attitudes toward life and the world. At one end of the spectrum we find what can be called trivializing postmodernity. The currents of trivializing postmodernity emphasize the extent to which the construction of patterns of life are based not on certain knowledge but on chance and decisions made in situations of uncertainty. They highlight the fact that the more we come to realize that universal understanding is not achievable, the more likely it is that we may be forced to accept a quite limited sense of what we can hope for in our personal and communal lives. They promote skepticism and at times even nihilistic critique, especially toward any broad or inclusive claims about the potential of human thought and activity. They encourage a rejection of optimistic modern notions of progress and development. Such notions are to be replaced by a feel for social power and the realization that social life inevitably involves wins and losses, as those with differing views of life struggle to gain control of the processes of socially constructing knowledge.

Postmodern irony and wounded postmodernism are two forms of trivializing postmodernity frequently found today. Jedediah Purdy captures postmodern irony when he writes:

> The ironic individual practices a style of speech and behavior that avoids all appearance of naivete—of naïve devotion, belief, or hope. He subtly protests the inadequacy of the things he says, the gestures he makes, the acts he performs. By the inflection of his voice, the expression of his face, and the motion of his body, he signals that he is aware of all the ways he may be thought silly or jejune, and that he might even think so himself.[16]

The postmodern ironist continues to make use of modern modes of speech and action. At the same time, he or she acknowledges the postmodern critique of the grand claims of modernity and accepts a postmodern sense that life is much more limited, more trivial than modernity would lead us to believe.

Wounded postmodernism, a phenomenon described by Joseph Feeney, is similar to postmodern irony. The wounded postmodernist also accepts the postmodern critique of modernity and the sense that life possibilities are really quite finite and fragile. However, the wounded postmodernist questions whether it is really worth trying to make sense of life or the world anymore. In taking the postmodern critique to the extreme, wounded postmodernism results in "a sense of exhaustion, a loss of feeling and meaning, minimal expectations, and hopes, and a desire to parody everything."[17]

Questing postmodernism lies at the other end of the spectrum from trivializing postmodernity. Questing postmodernists seek to replace the modern Age of Enlightenment with what might be called an Age of Candor and/or an Age of Pragmatic Action. On the one hand, questing postmodernists generally accept the postmodern critique of modernity. They tend to reject hopes of beginning with universal understanding; accept the specificity, contingency, and limitation of human knowledge; and may acknowledge the realities of social power. On the other hand, rather than seeing the currents of postmodernity as a burden that trivializes life, questers (sometimes reluctantly and at other times wholeheartedly) see postmodernity as an opportunity. From the questing perspective, postmodernity provides us with the chance to be more open, honest, and candid about ourselves and the world than we could be in the past.

Building upon a candid critique of life and the world, postmodern questers generally seek to promote imaginative creativity and the pragmatic construction of new patterns of self-identity and social solidarity. For questers, the postmodern agenda culminates in freedom to envision and embrace new, more life-giving and life-enhancing ways of being. Questers promote a hope in the future that is more guarded and cautiously expressed than the hope of modernity. At the same time, postmodern questers strive to reach beyond the limitations of modernity by grounding aspirations for the future in a more realistic sense of both the achievements and limitations of the past.[18]

Now, cultural shifts always meet resistance. A comprehensive account of emerging cultural postmodernity would explore the uneven surfaces of this cultural shift in greater detail and examine the various ways it has been resisted and reacted against. However, the background provided here can enable us to begin to recognize how postmodernity is affecting the church.

Cultural Postmodernity and the Church

The currents of cultural postmodernity are at one and the same time diminishing and enlivening Christian faith communities today. On the one hand, Christians who absorb trivializing postmodernity tend to move beyond or to the fringe of the church. The church becomes one of the large institutions they regard with suspicion or even contempt. On the other hand, the currents of questing post-modernity are flowing through the doors of church buildings, parish halls, schools, homes, and other Christian faith-centered institutions today. These currents tend to sweep away the modern search for enlightenment, replacing it with postmodern candor and a pragmatic spiritual quest to find new, more authentic ways of connecting with God, self, and others.

The postmodern spiritual questers found within the church can be divided into two main groups. The largest of these is made up of those who can be called reluctant postmodernists. Pushed by the complexities and ambiguities of contemporary life, reluctant postmodernists slowly, incrementally, and sometimes grudgingly move beyond overarching, inclusive, and foundational frameworks of meaning and value to accept the specificity, contingency, and limitation of all human knowing. However, once they experience the gestalt shift from a modern to a postmodern perspective, they begin to recognize the new possibilities and freedoms postmodernity has to offer.

Ann and her faith community provide a paradigmatic example of the spiritual questing of reluctant postmodernists. Ann has been working at a parish in southern Minnesota for almost fifteen years, a parish with a large Hispanic presence. The chicken farms and processing plants have brought in a lot of workers from Mexico, Latin

92

America, and South America. During her years of ministry in southern Minnesota Ann has seen the parish she serves go from being rural and Anglo (mostly German) to become a diverse, multicultural, suburban faith community.

When Ann reflects on how the parish she serves has changed, she charts four phases of development. The general attitude of the first phase is captured by the phrase *They are different from us.* As Hispanics/Latinos began to settle in the area, they tended to keep to themselves. The Anglos in turn kept their distance from the various Hispanic groups. There was a Spanish Mass for the Hispanics and a so-called regular, that is, English, Mass for the Anglos. During the second phase the sentiment shifted to *They are more like us than it seemed at first.* An awareness of common interests and concerns began to emerge at this time. During phase three the dominant theme became *We are all in this together.* There began to be a mixing of cultures. It became a common liturgical practice to have one verse of a song in English and another verse in Spanish. The underlying (modernist) assumptions of this phase were that Hispanic and Anglo cultures would eventually meld together into one, and that a unified and universalizing perspective would emerge from this melding.

The fourth phase, now emerging, bears all the marks of postmodern spiritual questing. This phase began when people started to realize that differences between and even among the Hispanics and Anglos would most likely always remain. Eventually, people began to admit that they valued the richness of having contrasting and at times even competing visions of Christian faith in their community. Acceptance of the realities of diversity sometimes promotes a freer and less rigid sense of community life. Finally, as they live with plural and multicultural attitudes and practices, many of the members of this community are learning to become comfortable with the fact that there can be many ways, both personally and socially, of embracing a life of Christian discipleship. Overall, Ann's faith community illustrates one way of addressing the growing pluralism that, according to recent sociological studies, now characterizes the majority of main-line Christian churches in the United States.[19]

Wholehearted postmodernists, the other major and growing group of spiritual questers in the contemporary church, stand in contrast to reluctant postmodernists. Moreover, wholehearted, Christian, postmodern spiritual questing is often expressed in a number of identifiable forms. First, it is sometimes marked by a religious eclecticism, a drawing together of spiritual resources from various Christian denominations or a combining of Christianity with insights and spiritual practices from other faith traditions. For instance, consider the faith quest of Jerry. Jerry is a very successful radio announcer. During a recent conversation Jerry turned to the subject of spirituality. He noted that all his life he has been able to connect with people, but what he really wants is to connect with God. In postmodern fashion Jerry candidly critiqued what he called the cold, aloof quality of most Christian liturgies. He also noted that the grand stories of salvation history he heard in church and school meant little to him. Jerry claimed that, for him, life is about individual people striving to overcome the alienation and fragmentation of the world by connecting with other people and with God. He added, "If enough connections can be made, community begins to form."

Jerry remains an active volunteer in his parish and says he attends Mass on Christmas and Easter because these parish connections help to meet his spiritual needs. He also noted that he has turned elsewhere in search of spiritual guidance. He practices yoga and Buddhist meditation. He is in a study group at a local meditation center to read, discuss, and meditate or pray with classic texts of Eastern spirituality. Jerry now describes himself as a Buddhist Catholic. He is not sure if yoga, Buddhist meditation, and involvement in a Catholic parish "all fit together somehow." Yet, he knows (pragmatically) that this combination works for him. There are increasing numbers of people like Jerry within or on the fringes of our faith communities today.

Second, an openness to faith experimentation sometimes characterizes wholehearted, postmodern, Christian spiritual questing. Such faith experimentation involves a willingness to adapt Christian beliefs and practices so that they address contemporary life situations more fully. Consider, as an example, the case of the Wilsons—Mark and Sally, and their teenage sons, Ben and Roger. For a number of years Ben and Roger have vocally expressed their dislike for Sunday Mass. Finally, Sally and Mark admitted to their sons that Sunday liturgy is sometimes less than a truly prayerful and meaningful experience for them as well.

Family discussions then led the Wilsons to create what they call home churching. Every other week, instead of attending Sunday Mass, the family has a special breakfast. They begin and end with prayer, and include a reading of the Christian scriptures for the day. As they enjoy their meal together, they talk about ways of connecting the insights gained from scripture with their everyday lives.

The Wilsons note that Christians have periodically reshaped the Sunday liturgy to meet their spiritual needs. They suggest that their home churching is an innovative practice developed to meet the spiritual needs of their family. They have explored traditions of Christian prayer and have used liturgical practices from past eras to shape the way they conduct their home-churching celebrations. They would like to bring the insights gained from their home churching back to their parish community, but they are not quite sure how to do this or that their parish/institutional church would welcome it.

Overall, there are increasing numbers of people within Christian faith communities who, influenced by the currents of cultural postmodernity, are experimenting with liturgy, prayer, rituals of forgiveness and reconciliation, and other Christian practices. While this faith experimentation is taking place, it is not often discussed or acknowledged openly in the church today. Those involved in faith experimentation may feel that they lack the social power to express their spiritual questing within the structures of the institutional church, or they may fear that the social power of the church might be used against them if they openly express their spiritual needs.

Third, in their spiritual questing wholehearted, postmodern Christians sometimes attempt to bypass religious traditions and institutional structures. For instance, I met Bradley when he asked me to be the institutional-church connection to a group he founded that was sponsoring a men's spirituality conference. (I then worked for the local Catholic diocese, and Brad wanted a connection with me primarily to give him access to the pastors in the diocese.) Displaying a postmodern distrust of institutions, Brad did not want his group's conference to be sponsored by the local diocese. He felt that an independent, open, questioning approach would attract more men and have greater credibility given what he described as "all the hang-ups in the hierarchical church."

Brad's witness talk at the conference was based on the phrase *W-W-J-D—What Would Jesus Do*. He spoke of the conference as an opportunity for men to connect with Jesus. He never mentioned the traditions or institutional structures of the church as sources of wisdom that could guide a believer to grow in relationship with Jesus. Like Microsoft's microserfs and many Christians I have met in the past twenty years, Brad regards large church institutions, with their traditions and denominational structures, as things that might occasionally be useful. Still, he believes that the real work (including spiritual work) gets done at the local level by individuals and small groups.

As the currents of reluctant and wholehearted postmodernity rise within the church, Christian faith communities are becoming more diverse. Moreover, this diversity is eliciting two patterns of response. On the one hand, it often spawns greater division. Some Christians regard with suspicion those who adopt a questing, postmodern faith stance. Postmodern spiritual questers may be accused of relativism, syncretism, or worse. In turn, some postmodern spiritual questioners may shrug and turn away from inclusive questions of meaning and value, choosing instead to focus on making sense of the realities of diversity in their local faith communities. Others may react by becoming more candid and vocal in their critiques of church life and more open in their wholehearted embrace of cultural post-modernity.

On the other hand, the growing diversity in the church has sparked a search for common ground. Recent sociological studies sug-gest that despite the diversity in perspectives in the church today, there remains a fair amount of agreement about the fundamental beliefs of Christian faith. Beyond divergences in perspective, those who continue to affiliate or identify in some way with the church most often reject the trivializing tendencies at the extreme end of emerging postmodern sensibilities and affirm the continuing impor-tance of authentic Christian faith and spirituality.[20]

Postmodernity and Christian Religious Education

Christian faith formation has always been a demanding yet rewarding task. An understanding of the currents of cultural post-modernity may make Christian religious education seem even more daunting and potentially less fulfilling. However, I suggest we view the currents of cultural postmodernity as providing an opportunity for renewal. I offer the following guidelines for taking advantage of this opportunity.

1. *Christian faith formation needs to highlight the value of the positive, quest-ing dimensions of emerging cultural postmodernity.*

The United States Catholic Conference (USCC) notes in *Our Hearts Were Burning Within Us* that "we live in a diverse multicultural society that offers us a rich experience of how the faith is lived, expressed, and celebrated in our own time." The USCC adds, "We are entering a period of new vitality for the Church." Our first response to the various forms of spiritual questing we find in the church today must be to welcome them as signs of "rich experience" and "new vitality."[21] They can then become starting points for the new evangelization.

Questing postmodernity offers a critique of modernity that does not sink into skepticism or cynicism. Rather, it strives candidly to question established ways of thinking and acting in order to create structures of meaning and value that are more appropriate for the fast-paced, multifarious era in which we now live. Christian religious educators can make a significant contribution to contemporary discussions about the meaning and value of life if we begin by taking seriously the contemporary postmodern spiritual questing we find in the church today.[22] We need to embrace the various forms of postmodern spiritual questing in their concrete specificity as genuine attempts to recognize and respond to the initiative of God in the world today.

2. *Ongoing religious education and adult faith formation need to become central to the life of Christian faith communities.*

Thirty years ago in *To Teach as Jesus Did* the National Conference of Catholic Bishops (NCCB) noted with great foresight that

> today, perhaps more than ever before, it is important to recognize that learning is a lifelong experience. Rapid, radical changes in contemporary society demand well planned, continuing efforts to assimilate new data, new insights, new modes of thinking and acting. This is necessary for adults to function efficiently, but, more important, to achieve full realization of their potential as persons whose destiny includes but also transcends this life.[23]

Present-day youth and young adults, members of the Millennial Generation and Generation X, have never known anything but the fast-paced, ever-changing world of cultural postmodernity. For many in these generations, the Second Vatican Council and the shift from a classical to a modern worldview seem like ancient history.

Generally, they recognize the necessity of well-planned, continuing efforts to address the ever-new ways of thinking and acting of our age. Faith communities that stress the importance of ongoing religious education and adult faith formation (rather than the presentation of an already formulated Christian meta-narrative) are likely to have the potential to attract and hold the attention of Millennials and Gen X-ers.

Those of us from the Baby Boom Generation or older (that is, those of us born before the early 1960s) grew to maturity in an age very different from the present one. Many of us were taught to think of religious education as something that ended with the sacrament of confirmation or twelfth-grade religious-education class—unless, of course, we decided to "enter the religious life." Today, we need to recognize that just as we may develop and change emotionally, psychologically, and socially as our lives unfold, we have the potential to grow in our relationship with God and ability to relate our faith to our everyday lives. As the pace of cultural change accelerates, we must also recognize the need for ongoing faith formation that enables us to relate our Christian faith to the complexities and ambiguities of our ever-changing postmodern world.

3. *The resources of Christian faith traditions need to be used to foster critical reflection and evaluation of emerging postmodern practices.*

Critical engagement with the currents of cultural postmodernity needs to be central to present-day Christian faith formation efforts. Christian affirmations of the goodness of God's creation and the dignity of the human person as made in the image and likeness of God can provide a basis for combating the forces of trivializing postmodernity. Just as important, while we need to affirm the legitimacy of postmodern spiritual questing, there are often ways that the resources of Christian traditions can be used to invite questers to a deeper, richer faith. For instance, those who have turned to Eastern religious practices to enrich their faith are sometimes tempted to adopt a "too easy" or facile combining of Christian and Eastern religious practices. If provided with opportunities to explore both the similarities and differences among Christian and other religious traditions, they may be invited beyond an unnuanced and untenable eclecticism.[24]

4. *In our postmodern age, community formation needs to become central to religious educational efforts.*

Pope John Paul II, in his 1989 apostolic exhortation on the lay faithful, wrote of the need for the "formation of mature ecclesial communities."[25] Similarly, the GDC notes that

> continuing formation in faith is directed not only to the individual Christian...but also to the Christian community as such so that it may mature also in its interior life of love of God and of the brethren as well as in its openness to the world as a missionary community. (no. 70)

The formation of Christian congregations as communities of learning needs to become central to Christian faith formation.

Today, Christian community formation has become more difficult as postmodern fragmentation affects the life of the church. At one end of the spectrum, some Christians are drawn to one or another form of sectarianism. They retreat from the broader world, seeking solace from the currents of postmodern complexity in either the uniqueness of biblical revelation and inerrancy, or the teachings of the hierarchical magisterium as *the* expression of the wisdom of Christian tradition. At the other end of the spectrum, those who are distrustful of the church as an institution and who move to the margins of the church sometimes launch destructively angry critiques of Church life and practices. The vast majority of the church, standing between these two extremes, can feel caught or attacked from both sides. While we may be accused by those with a sectarian bent of being unorthodox or lacking "true belief," we may at the same time be charged with being overly conservative or rigid by those moving more deeply into the deconstructive and critically reflective dimensions of postmodern culture. After defending ourselves against internal attackers, we are often left without the energy to use the resources of Christian faith traditions to address the pressing postmodern issues of our day. Additionally, the internal struggles that come to plague the church because of the influence of those at the extreme ends of the spectrum of Christian faith often lead our faith communities to become yet another casualty of, rather than an antidote to, the corrosive acids of trivializing postmodernity.

To counter the social fragmentation both within and beyond the church, faith formation efforts need to promote the formation of mature ecclesial communities that can respond to the currents of emerging cultural postmodernity. Specifically, within Christian faith communities today there needs to be opportunities for dialogue or conversation about the ways cultural postmodernity is shaping our understandings of morality, our senses of personal and social identity, and our outlooks on life and the world. Christians with differing theological stances need to be able to present their views while at the same time remaining respectful of those with whom they disagree. Through such dialogue those who emphasize the importance of Christian scripture and tradition may be able to help wholehearted spiritual questers develop a renewed appreciation for the resources found within Christian faith traditions. In turn, spiritual questers may challenge sectarian tendencies by affirming a basic Christian belief that God remains actively involved in the world, that God continues to reveal God's self within the joys and hopes, struggles and anxieties of our day—including the hopes and anxieties of emerging cultural postmodernity. To the extent that there is genuine conversation about important contemporary issues, Christians may be able to root their communal lives more fully in prayerful openness to God and discernment of what God is requiring and enabling us to do as we strive to address the currents of cultural change.

5. Spirituality needs to be a central focus in Christian religious education for a postmodern age.

"I'm spiritual but not religious" is a common postmodern refrain. In making such a comment, the speaker most often wants to express interest in deepening a relationship with God and affirming the transcendent dimension of human personality. At the same time, such a comment often expresses a distancing from or even distrust of the institutional church and a lack of affiliation with a Christian faith community.

As we move more fully into postmodernity, the church needs to affirm, even honor, the spiritual questing of our age. We need to be open to recognizing the initiative of God in our lives and world as we delve into the rising currents of cultural postmodernity. Christian beliefs, liturgical practices, and communal life need to be viewed in terms of whether or not they contribute to nurturing people's sense of spirituality. Christian religious education as a whole may even be re-envisioned as an activity within the larger ambit of nurturing spirituality; that is, as an activity whose primary purpose is to contribute to a greater sense of spiritual meaning and value on both personal and communal levels. Moreover, Christian faith communities need to reach out to those on the borders or beyond their faith communities by offering the resources of Christian faith traditions to nurture their spiritual growth.

At the same time, Christian religious education must also critique some aspects of emerging postmodern spirituality. A spirituality disconnected from a faith community can too easily become a privatized or small-group expression of faith that is forgetful of the collective wisdom of Christian traditions or neglectful of the Christian mission to welcome and work to bring about the fuller realization of the values of God's reign, God's peace and justice, within the world. Overall, while encouraging the spiritual enthusiasm emerging within postmodernity, the church must also emphasize the importance of membership in a faith community and outreach to the broader world as essential dimensions of a mature Christian spirituality.

6. A feel for the currents of cultural postmodernity can lead religious educators to place renewed emphasis today on Christian moral formation.

The currents of cultural postmodernity have made the waters of morality murkier. Postmodernity has heightened our awareness of the ways moral values are not just discovered, but are constructed by persons and communities within specific life contexts and are never fully expressive of an objective moral order. As we move more fully into postmodernity we are also likely to encounter competing and conflicting moral visions and values within and among our families, faith communities, places of employment, and various other social structures of which we are a part.

At the same time, the positive dimensions of postmodern sensibilities often lead today to a heightened awareness of the moral dimensions of life. First, a greater sense of personal moral responsibility can emerge from a postmodern emphasis on our role as moral agents in constructing an understanding of the world and then taking responsibility for what we have created. Second, postmodern questioning of large institutions and sensitivity to the dynamics of social power can lead to a renewed sense of social morality. When people come to the conclusion that existing institutional structures cannot always be counted upon to address social issues fairly, there may be an increased commitment to respond to contemporary concerns about social justice.

Christian faith formation efforts can draw from the resources of Christian traditions to address both the moral challenges and opportunities presented by emerging cultural postmodernity. Christian faith traditions provide insightful explorations of the moral dimensions of personal and social life, detailed analysis of ethical issues in business, medicine, and other professional arena, and rich reflections on the nature of moral character, integrity, and virtue. In our increasingly postmodern world there may be an openness to the wisdom of Christian faith if the resources of Christian faith traditions are presented not as definitive moral pronouncements linked to an all-inclusive Christian meta-narrative but as contributions to ongoing discussions about how to construct meaningful and morally responsible patterns of personal and social life today.

Notes

1. The distinction between philosophical postmodernism and cultural postmodernity is taken from Michael Paul Gallagher, *Clashing Symbols* (New York: Paulist Press, 1998), 87. Paul Lakeland offers a useful introduction to issues of cultural postmodernity and Christian faith in *Postmodernity: Christian Identity in a Fragmented Age* (Minneapolis: Fortress Press, 1997). Stanley Grenz, ed., *A Primer on Postmodernism* (Grand Rapids, Mich.: Eerdmans, 1996), provides an overview of philosophical postmodernism. Those interested in the possible intersection of postmodernism and Christian theology should see Merold Westphal, ed., *Postmodern Philosophy and Christian Thought* (Bloomington, Ind.: Indiana University Press, 1999).

2. On Generation X, see Geoffrey T. Holtz, *Welcome to the Jungle: The Why Behind 'Generation X'* (New York: St. Martin's Press, 1995), and Neil Howe and Bill Strauss, *Thirteenth Generation* (New York: Vintage Books, 1993). On Christian faith and Generation X, see Tom Beaudoin, *Virtual Faith: The Irreverent Spiritual Quest of Generation X* (San Francisco: Jossey-Bass, 1998) and Beaudoin's essay in this collection. On the Millennial Generation, see Neil Howe and Bill Strauss, *Millennials Rising* (New York: Vintage Press, 2000). Generation X consists of the age cohort born between the early to mid 1960s and the early to mid 1980s. The Millennial Generation includes the cohort born from the early to mid 1980s to the present.

3. Walter Truett Anderson, *Reality Isn't What It Used to Be* (San Francisco: Harper & Row, 1990), 75.

4. An insightful theological exploration of the shift from a classical to a modern worldview is supplied by Bernard Lonergan in "Theology in Its New Context," in *Theology of Renewal*, Vol. 1, *Renewal of Religious Thought*, ed. L. K. Shock (New York: Herder and Herder, 1968), 34–46; and "The Transition from a Classical World-View to Historical Mindedness," in *Law for Liberty*, ed. James E. Biechler (Baltimore: Helican Press, 1967), 126–33.

5. See the introduction to Jean-Francois Lyotard, *The Postmodern Condition* (Minneapolis: University of Minnesota Press, 1984).

6. For example, see Richard Rorty, "Solidarity or Objectivity," in *Post-Analytic Philosophy*, ed. John Rajchman and Cornel West (New York: Columbia University Press, 1985).

7. For an example of this stance, see the chapter "Tradition and Genealogy" in Alasdair MacIntyre, *Three Rival Versions of Moral Enquiry* (Notre Dame, Ind.: University of Note Dame Press, 1990). MacIntyre accepts the postmodern critique of modernity but sees himself as offering an alternative to philosophical postmodernism. MacIntyre's work builds upon a reaction against the currents of postmodernity in the broader culture.

8. Michel Foucault and Jacques Derrida, considered by many to be the paradigmatic postmodern philosophers, each contributes in his own way to our understanding of the socially created or constructed nature of knowledge. Foucault's philosophical project was to explore the finite, situated dimensions of human understanding in such areas as mental illness, knowledge production, and sexuality. Foucault's analysis strips away any illusions that our sense of self can be separated from our social context. Foucault's approach to philosophical enquiry is outlined in his essay "What Is Enlightenment?" in *The Foucault Reader*, ed. Paul Rabinow (New York: Pantheon Books, 1984). Derrida's project is to subvert or deconstruct our taken-for-granted understandings so that we might recognize more fully how our views are embedded in interpretive structures of meaning that are always open to re-evaluation. While Derrida's writings are quite dense and difficult, a fairly clear introduction to his thought is provided in *Deconstruction in a Nutshell: A Conversation with Jacques Derrida*, ed. John Caputo (New York: Fordham University Press, 1997).

9. Although he does not use the term *postmodern*, William E. Diehl explores the kinds of question about Christian identity that are being raised with increasing frequency today (see especially his *The Monday Connection* [San Francisco: Harper, 1991] and *Ministry in Daily Life* [Washington, D.C.: The Alban Institute, 1996]).

10. A postmodern analysis of a de-centered and fragmentary sense of self-identity is provided by Jacques Lacan (see, for example, his *The Four Fundamental Concepts of Psychoanalysis*, trans. Alan Sheridan [London: Penguin, 1979] and *Ecritis: A Selection*, trans. Alan Sheridan [London: Tavistock, 1977]).

11. Roderick Firth and Arthur J. Dyck provide examples of modern approaches to understanding morality in which an effort to achieve foundational and comprehensive knowledge becomes centrally important (see Firth, "Ethical Absolutism and the Ideal Observer," *Philosophy and Phenomenological Research* 12, no. 3 [March 1952]: 317–45; and Dyck, "Moral Requiredness: Bridging the Gap Between 'Ought' and 'Is,'" Part 1,

The Journal of Religious Ethics 6, no. 2 [1978]: 293–318, and Part 2, *The Journal of Religious Ethics* 9, no. 1 [1981]: 525–45).

12. A critique of modern conceptions of morality following this line of argument is found in Alasdair MacIntyre, *Whose Justice? Which Rationality?* (Notre Dame, Ind.: University of Notre Dame Press, 1990).

13. The archeological image is taken from Michel Foucault, *The Order of Things: An Archeology of the Human Sciences* (New York: Vintage Books, 1970).

14. The lives of microserfs are parodied in Douglas Coupland's novel *Microserfs* (London: Flamingo, 1995).

15. An analysis of the role of power in social life is central to Foucault's work (see *Discipline and Punish: The Birth of the Prison,* trans. Alan Sheridan [New York: Pantheon Books, 1977], and *Power/Knowledge: Selected Interviews and Other Writings, 1972–1977,* ed. Colin Gordon [New York: Random House, 1977]).

16. Jedediah Purdy, *For Common Things: Irony, Trust, and Commitment in America Today* (New York: Knopf, 1999), xi.

17. Joseph J. Feeney, "Can a Worldview be Healed? Students and Postmodernism," *America* 177, 13, 1997.

18. Both Derrida and Foucault can be interpreted as seeking, ultimately, to contribute to a positive, questing sense of postmodernism in philosophy (see John D. Caputo, *The Prayers and Tears of Jacques Derrida* [Bloomington, Ind.: Indiana University Press, 1997] and James W. Bernauer, *Michel Foucault's Force of Flight* [Atlantic Highlands, N.J.: Humanities Press International, 1990]). At the level of popular culture examples of trivializing and questing postmodernity abound. For instance, a few years ago the highest-rated television show, *Seinfeld,* a show about "nothing" or a group of people who lead trivial "do nothing" lives, served as a paradigm example of the negative, nihilistic pole of postmodernity. In contrast, *Touched by an Angel,* the second-highest-rated television show at the time, exemplified the postmodern quest to find the spiritual resources to take a candid look at and then renew one's life. In popular films Matt Stone and Trey Parker's *South Park* illustrates a trivializing of the power of language, the importance of relationships, and the meaning of social life. In contrast, the character Jack Dawson (portrayed by Leonardo DiCaprio) in James Cameron's *Titanic* exemplifies the candid, restless, adventurous, yet ultimately hopeful spirit of questing postmodernity. Douglas Coupland's novel *Life After God* (New York: Pocket Books, 1994) explores both the trivializing and questing dynamics of postmodern cultures for Gen-Xers reaching mid-life. One of the best examples of quest-

ing postmodernity in popular culture is found in J. K. Rowling's Harry Potter series of books.

19. The story of Ann's faith community was told to me by Jane Regan.
20. The greater diversity yet underlying unity within present-day American Catholicism is discussed in James D. Davidson et al., *The Search for Common Ground* (Huntington, Ind.: Our Sunday Visitor, 1997) and William V. D'Antonio et al., *Laity, American and Catholic* (Kansas City, Mo.: Sheed and Ward, 1996). See also Dean Hoge et al., *Young Adult Catholics: Religion in the Culture of Choice* (Notre Dame, Ind.: University of Notre Dame Press, 2001).
21. United States Catholic Conference, *Our Hearts Were Burning Within Us* (Washington, D.C.: USCC, 1999), 1.
22. The work of Leonard Sweet is somewhat helpful in understanding how Christian religious education needs to adapt to postmodern culture (see especially *Post-Modern Pilgrims* [Nashville, Tenn.: Broadman & Holman, 2000] and *SoulTsunami: Sink or Swim in New Millennium Culture* [Grand Rapids, Mich.: Zondervan, 1999]).
23. National Conference of Catholic Bishops, *To Teach as Jesus Did* (Washington, D.C.: USCC, 1973), no. 43.
24. For a similar point, see Tom Beaudoin's suggestion in his essay in this collection that the traditions of the church be taught as a toolbox for discerning sin and grace in popular media culture and everyday life.
25. John Paul II, *Apostolic Exhortation on the Vocation and the Mission of the Lay Faithful in the Church and in the World (Christifideles Laici), Origins* 18 (9 February 1989), no. 34.

6

Mysticism—God's Initiative and Our Response

Maryanne Confoy

As we look to the future of religious education and imagine new possibilities for the church's ministry of faith education in family, parish, and school, I propose that the new growth area of adult faith will be in our efforts to take seriously God's initiative in our faith journey. Thomas Groome's invitation to "reject religious education that does not engage and affect people's very 'being'—who they are and how they live"[1] acknowledges the importance of a catechetical approach that is "total" in its impact on people's lives, and in its connectedness to the Christian faith heritage. In the past decade particularly, researchers have explored the gamut of approaches to spirituality, from sacred to secular. Colleen Griffith reminds us that the eclectic and inclusive term *spirituality* is displacing the exclusiveness of institutional *religion* in bookstores and in everyday conversations.[2]

Yet spirituality has its own integrity and its own interpretive sources. While the generic and most inclusive understanding of the term may be "the experience of trying to integrate one's life in terms of self-transcendence toward the ultimate value one perceives,"[3] there are many variations across religious traditions. From a *Christian* perspective, spirituality has been described as "who one really is, the deepest self, not entirely accessible to the most thoughtful self-scrutiny and reflection...God's salvation in Christ and the response of individuals and groups to that salvation."[4] Such a description emphasizes the personal efforts of Christians who strive to be faithful to their God and to their religious beliefs. Humans need to have a purpose for living, and Christian spirituality gives specific meaning and purpose to people's beliefs and values. As educators and communicators of the Christian faith we are concerned with enabling people to become more consciously aware of the lifelong task of shaping their lives in accord with their chosen beliefs and values.

Yet, aware as we are of the importance of our own efforts, over time we can become even more aware of the significance of God's initiative in our lives. Adult faith education in the next several years may well give priority to developing people's awareness of the primacy of God's activity in our mutual loving relationships. Thus while spirituality describes *our* efforts to reach out to God, mysticism emphasizes *God's* initiative in reaching out to us in and through the ordinary and extraordinary experiences of our lives. It is important, then, for us to enable people to have an understanding of, and a language for, this aspect of their faith life. It is also helpful for us to ask in what ways certain religious experiences and ways of connecting with God have been sanctioned and what experiences have been marginalized or lost because they do not fit into the normative patterns and expectations of the Christian communities to which we belong.

How can we discount or ignore what has been a significant component of our living Christian tradition? As the mystical journey does not originate from our efforts but from God's initiative, who are we to set up the boundaries for possible recipients of God's special gifts—ourselves included? Tom Beaudoin's emphasis on the revitalizing of the religious imagination alerts readers to the readiness of young adults "to take more risks in relating to God and in imaging their spiritual development."[5] Professional religious educators may need to take similar risks if their catechetical activities are to connect

110

with the inner world and aspirations of young adults today. If we believe that our love for God depends only on our efforts, we may not be able to discern God's invitation to contemplative union. Our convictions about our own unworthiness, or about God's way of reaching out to people, may render us deaf to God's loving invitations. If our focus is on ourselves rather than on the unconditionally loving God who calls us to deeper levels of union, then we will miss those moments of graced potential!

The worlds of consumerism and materialism have left many Westerners not simply with the psychic "numbness" described by Robert Jay Lifton, but also with a *spiritual overload*.[6] Such an overload can lead people to become observers and consumers of, rather than participants in, life and relationships. People can simply live passively on life's surface and deny the reality and energies of their inner world.

Christianity has a strong foundation of spiritual theology that has taken the inner world, the asceticism of contemplation or mystical union, seriously.[7] However, the associations of mysticism with florid descriptions of rapture, levitation, ecstasies, stigmata, and other extraordinary gifts have been prominent in the past, and they have frightened most Christians away from any notion of mystical potential in themselves. But traditional Christian authors see such paranormal phenomena as *secondary* mystical experiences.[8]

In the past decades there has been a shift in emphasis and in the approach to mysticism through the work of writers such as Thomas Merton, David Steindl Rast, Ruth Burrows, Rowan Williams, and William Johnston—to mention just a few of the significant contributors to our present-day understanding of mysticism. These writers have enabled their readers to gain contemporary understandings of mystical experiences as expressed in such English-language classics as William James, *The Varieties of Religious Experience* (1902), Evelyn Underhill, *Mysticism* (1911), and Cuthbert Butler, *Western Mysticism* (1922). Following the pioneering survey by Ronald Knox, *Enthusiasm* (1950), most more recent writers have avoided describing abstract mystical experience in favor of contextualizing such experiences in those cultural frameworks that channel the articulation of whatever it was that the mystic experienced. The "timeless" mystical encounter is now reinserted into time frames, so the cultural and historical influences that contributed to the way the experience was described and interpreted are more clearly recognized. Recent scholars who have explored the wide range of ways in which people experience God's gifting presence now describe the mystic not as "a special kind of human being" but rather see "every human being is a special kind of mystic."[9] This fits Rahner's theological affirmation of an everyday mysticism.[10] Mysticism has been described as loving knowledge or even as "radical fidelity to the demands of daily life, even if only through implicit, hidden or anonymous faith, hope and love—in self-surrender to the Mystery that haunts one's life."[11] This is the mysticism of daily life.

Why should we be interested in mysticism in daily life? To speak of mysticism in our daily lives is important

> because of God's *universal* self-communication, a communication that the human person must freely accept or reject, anyone—even the agnostic or atheist—who lives moderately, selflessly, honestly, courageously, and in silent service to others experiences the mysticism of daily life. The courageous, total acceptance of life and oneself, even when everything tangible seems to be collapsing, is perhaps the primary mystical experience of everyday life.[12]

God connects with us in the ordinariness of our human experiences, and we sense God's loving presence often without being able to use words to describe such experiences. The importance of our inner world in the experience of healing and being healed is affirmed by clinician Herbert Benson, who proposes that "our genetic blueprint has made believing in an Infinite Absolute part of our nature....Humans are wired for God!"[13] The consequence of this connectedness is that we all experience, as human beings, within the deepest dimensions of our being, the invitation, whether vaguely or implicitly, of God's self-communication in grace, of God reaching into our lives and touching us. However we experience it, whether as a recurrent restlessness of our hearts, a sense of unexplained "connectedness," or even a holy "dis-ease," it is the sense that we are part of something far larger than ourselves and our own immediate interests, and it can hit us at most unexpected times and in unexpected ways. We need to be attentive to such experiences of connectedness. Groome rejects any notion of a "docile reception of 'the faith'" and reminds us that our pedagogy "should reflect God's pedagogy over time." Such a pedagogy is both "active and participative," requiring a "conscious and co-responsible" (GDC, no. 167) attentiveness to our own "lived experience" (GDC, no. 152c).[14] Such a pedagogy is a mystical pedagogy in which our God takes the initiative.

Mystical experience is one expression of the graced life that we have all been invited to live as human beings. For Christians, this graced life is a consequence of baptism, and it has an impact on our awareness of God. Spiritual writers make a distinction between the various levels and styles of our ways of relating with our God.[15] Perhaps the most important issue here, in relation to mysticism, is that the higher levels of union with God, or "infused contemplation," are not the consequence of our personal desires and efforts. They are the fruit of God's loving activity in us. It is through God's initiative that we can become more explicitly aware of God's presence and of our response.

Although in the past such understandings of mysticism and prayer were attributed to a religious elite, this can no longer be the case. John of the Cross claimed that the mystical journey is for the ordinary person and "dark night" experiences are not the prerogative of spiritual giants. John wrote for all people who are taking their inner life seriously, or at least endeavoring to do so. Christians today are still dealing with the fears and inhibitions of the nineteenth- and early-twentieth-century hierarchical communities, where there was a much more elitist understanding of the mystical way.[16] The mystical journey is not a topic preached from most pulpits, or one that educators have been encouraged to address in their curriculum. However, there is a prevailing concern among spiritual writers in today's frenetic world to reclaim the contemplative dimension of life. Many good books have been written on this. But it is also important to acknowledge explicitly the mystical element intrinsic to this endeavor, or the integral relationship between the God of love and the person praying will be subordinated to the science of contemplation. The "know how" is important in contemplative prayer, but God's gratuitous initiative, rather than our acquisition of "skills," is the essence of Christian mysticism. Through baptism all Christians are called to mystical contemplation.[17] Mystical contemplation is not extraordinary; it is very ordinary. Christians who follow this path become their most authentic selves.[18]

To illustrate this, let me give you a scenario of the spiritual journey with which we are all probably familiar. Most of us, if asked who we are, would describe ourselves as Mary or John Citizen, fairly ordinary people, important to our family, to a few friends, and perhaps to the communities to which we belong as educators and/or worshipers. At our best we are effective religious professionals and "do-gooders"; at our worst we are as selfish or as vindictive or as struggling with forgiveness as our neighbor is likely to be. We have a reasonable degree of self-knowledge and freedom in our lives. Then, something totally unexpected might happen to us—an accident, a major illness, a significant relationship beginning or closing, even a birthday that suddenly confronts us with some of life's big questions. What is the meaning of my life? Do I have any significance—for anyone—even for myself? When these uneasy and disturbing questions catch up with us our self-assurance drops and our doubts rise to the surface. Sometimes we are confronted with feelings of anger, despair, doubt, confusion, and fear. If we allow ourselves to experience these feelings and do not run away from them or repress them, it is possible for us to move to a deeper level of self-knowledge and greater compassion for others in their struggles for meaning.

Our daily life consistently triggers events that call our personal projects and emotional programs for security and happiness into question. From such experiences comes the possibility of more intensive and expansive horizons of meaning for our own lives, and for life in general. Our inner world receives more attention at these times. We do not set out to be mystics, but we find ourselves drawn into a depth of living and loving that seems to be out of our own control and power to predict. Under God's palpable initiative and direction, we may find ourselves becoming more deeply aware of God's love and presence, sometimes abruptly, other times gradually. Through God's special activity, we become aware that God is in love with us, and therefore we are called, in some foundational way, to respond in love to God and experience connectedness with one another. "The explicit awareness of God's burning love at the very roots of their being causes mystics an immense longing that allows them no peace until they are irrevocably united to God and transformed into God's very own life."[19]

Many of us feel that longing, that ache for something other than what we have, but we don't know how to express our emptiness or our restlessness. We long to understand ourselves more, to have greater freedom in our lives, and to reach out to others in compassion, but we are fearful of what such desires might mean. Sometimes we take a risk; we venture forward, and we fall on our face! It is often at these times when we experience "failure" that God breaks through the comfortable structures we have built as "good" Christians and opens us up to new ways of authentic living and loving. This may take place through an immense longing in our hearts that can lead us to the mystical horizon of transforming engagement with God and the created world. What follows uses the classical three stages of the mystical journey and the experience of the dark night analyzed by John of the Cross (1542–91) to explore "everyday mysticism."

The Purgative Way: Confronted with Our Inner World

We enter the first stage of the mystical journey,[20] described as the purgative way,[21] by moving from a previous satisfaction with life, from a settledness in our lives, to a new sense of dissatisfaction or frustration with ourselves and our ways of relating. As adults in our varied social groups we long for companionship and understanding. We can find ourselves looking more skeptically at our relationships without knowing why. Our lives, which may have previously seemed comfortable and rewarding to us, take on a monochromatic dullness and drabness. This expresses the beginning of the purgative way. Sometimes we are confronted with the irony of our "loveless" love of God. When we experience God's action in our lives we experience our ambivalence.

> When God breaks in, my picture of what it is to be *me*, and my attitudes to that picture, have been deeply disturbed and confused. I am nearer than before to some sort of truthfulness, and I am plunged into confusion. Here is *God*, then, in the event that attacks and upsets my self-image, and so confuses the whole of my speech and imagery. [22]

Experiences of limitations, of aging and of illness, can also confront devout Christians with new questions. There can be a profound tastelessness for prayer and spiritual things. Bewilderment, despair, darkness, anger and confusion characterize this purgative stage—a stage where, paradoxically, one is growing closer to one's God while experiencing only distance and isolation. But it is not a growth through "warm and fuzzy" feelings of love or holiness but through the developing awareness of the emptiness of so many of the things into which we have put so much of our energy. Any satisfaction previously received through our prayer, our devotions, and our ministry has disappeared. Such negative feelings reverberate in a culture where many question whether it is worth trying to make sense of life any more. Religious educators cannot remain aloof from, or be untouched by, the philosophical and cultural questions and issues of our time.

We do not have a "desert" experience, but rather we become the deserted environment in which so much of our life is seen as dried up and without vitality. Our former comfortable self-image now feels boring and tarnished. We begin to see how insignificant our life has been. We find ourselves questioning the way we have lived out our relationships, our commitments, our life choices and directions. We find ourselves doing things through routine rather than commitment, because our efforts seem pointless and empty. Sometimes we persevere in our religious "duties" because these can become an anchor of faithfulness in the sea of doubts and questioning. The purgative way can be experienced as a consistent confrontation with our limitations that may endure for several months or even years. Alternatively we may experience times of storms of disillusionment or discomfort swamping us and disturbing our patterns of relating followed by relatively calm and stable periods. At times we may feel totally alone, and at other times we may unexpectedly receive an inner affirmation that gives us strength to go on and the courage to hope that there is some purpose in our life.

These inner challenges do not make sense to Christians who believe they have been faithful to God. Having done "the right thing," it seems quite unfair that they are faced with their limitations. They can continue to operate effectively on the surface, but their inner world is disturbed. Yet these reactions are usually an indication of spiritual awakening rather than failure. In describing the spirituality of the educator, Griffith uses Parker Palmer's metaphor of "the inner landscape of the teaching self." She describes some occasions when people experience teaching as "a repeated exercise in vulnerability" involving "failing, "bumbling" and "poverty of spirit."[23] Such painful periods may well be contemporary examples of the purgative way for educators.

Previous feelings that we had something to offer to others are gradually replaced by a sense of lack of purpose and a lack of self-worth. This is described as "interior darkness."[24] Experiences of consolation in good works or in prayer may have centered on ourselves and our feelings of satisfaction. During this interior darkness we begin to understand how much we relied on ourselves and our achievements in the past, even while we were affirming our trust in God through prayer and performance of our religious duties. It is a slow process to realize how much of our trust has been placed in ourselves and how little our trust has been in our God. The dark night is truly a time of purification at all levels of our being-in-relationship.

Many of us, as religious professionals, have learned through the years to exercise our ministry from positions of power and control, even in our prayer. In times of darkness we may find ourselves reviewing our lives in new ways. The prayer we learned to be faithful to over the years, discursive prayer or meditation, no longer seems fruitful. Try as we might to meditate on the scriptures, to place ourselves in a gospel scene, we feel increasingly dry and desolate. In our ministry, as we emphasize the importance of prayer, we can find ourselves feeling more and more like the hypocrites denounced by Jesus in the gospels. Yet our dryness is caused by the Holy Spirit leading us away from words and images into a new way of simply being present to God in the prayer of loving regard. This affects every level of our being and relating, not just our prayer life. New ways of living and loving together often have to be worked on as we confront and question other aspects of our lives.[25]

The purgative way enables us to break through the false self[26] that we have learned to construct from infancy onward. The false self performs in order to meet other people's expectations, or it is our mask of protectiveness—keeping others away from our true identity. We Christians talk a lot about love, but many of us have learned to live without it. There are Christians who have lived for years in functional relationships in which ordinary needs are met but there is no real sense of receiving from one another at any depth. Time can drain mutuality from our relationships. It is hard when people realize that the love they have held for others over the years is no longer reciprocated, or worse, that their love has been pragmatic and self-focused rather than an experience of mutual exchange.

The honest engagement with our disappointments and our doubts in our relationships with ourselves, with others, and with our God enables us to understand both the human and the divine aspects of our call to be loving human beings. It is a time of tough honesty with ourselves, when we are called to review and renegotiate our commitments and convictions. The purgative way is not for the sentimentalist in the spiritual journey. The fruit of honest and faithful commitment to our God is the awakening to a new stage of self-in-relationship. The purgative way confronts us with our reality, with our hopes and our pretenses in our inner world, and it opens us up to new possibilities of authentic believing, hoping, and loving.

But for some people the purgative way is too frightening. Those whose Christian faith commitment requires certainty and security reject the uncertainty of faith questions or doubts in their lives. When their "patterns of life" can no longer be based on "certain knowledge" or "universal understanding," their range of reactions moves from "skepticism" and "nihilistic critique" to "postmodern irony" and "wounded postmodernism."[27] Horell's descriptions encompass the range of attitudes we find in our contemporary Christian communities among both ministers and educators as well as in those they serve. Such attitudes may be contemporary examples of the spirituality of the dark night.

In an addictive society escape is only too easy. We can run away from the pain, from our fears, and from confrontation with our ambiguities and our pettiness. An alternative to accepting what is happening to us in this unexpected darkness is to move into a blaming mode. We may blame ourselves, our church, our families, or our friends for the pain that our inner world is generating. The invitation to grow in self-knowledge and faithfulness can be deflected into a focus on others. We can project our inner anxieties outward and become religious vigilantes of our communities, with our energies focused on accusation or condemnation of others rather than on self-awareness or self-acceptance. The inner disturbance of purgative awakening that was offered initially for growth can be twisted into religious fundamentalism and community divisiveness.

Those who are able to face their own illusions about themselves and their spiritual sufficiency have the courage to move into the next stage of the mystical journey.

The Illuminative Way:
Opening Up to the Darkness Within

Our journey through the purgative way leads us into a new and paradoxical way of experiencing God's loving presence in absence. The "ray of darkness"[28] of the illuminative way throws light on the self-centeredness to which, over the years, we have become blind. Purgative suffering has shattered our self-image, but this does not destroy us, because something new has come out of the experience. We become aware of a level of self-understanding and self-acceptance at the bedrock of our being, but it is not what we might have expected at earlier stages of our journey.[29]

Although there are protracted times when we feel we are going backward in the spiritual life, there are other periods when we sense, not power, but attunement with the creative rhythm of life. There is a new sense of God's presence, paradoxically, even in the experience of absence. We may have moments of intense communion interspersed with times of painful isolation. It is after experiences like these that we can sometimes proclaim that we have seen God. We don't mean we have seen a thing, or a face, or even a person. We mean we have been stopped in our tracks and turned inside out; we have experienced a process in which *we* are put in question at our deepest level. These can be experienced as "timeless" moments, sometimes fleeting and at other times quite protracted.

The passive night of spirit or the illuminative way leads us from earlier stages of self-preoccupation or self-satisfaction with *our* love for God to an authentic understanding that we are loved, not because we are good, but because God is loving. The focus moves from ourselves to God. This awakens an experience of genuine poverty of spirit in which we learn and accept that we have little to offer our God, but that God loves us for ourselves.

Self-acceptance and a new taste of closeness to God are fruits of this experience. Because this is a time of inner work, we begin to be attuned to new depths within us. It is a time when we often experience ourselves as divided, as being caught within dual value systems. We ask ourselves whether we are the "public self" we work so hard to project in company or the inner confusion of desires, fantasies, and so on that we try so hard to disown or repress. We are aware that the way other people see us can be quite different from how we see ourselves. Which of the two selves am I? The struggle between these two selves is real, and while they sometimes engage in dialogue, at other times they can be in conflict with each other. Our inner turmoil can be quite disturbing.

The dark-night experience throws a blinding light on our tensive value systems and on those aspects of our identity that have been generated from other people's expectations of us rather than from our inner truth. We experience our inner world as the battleground between good and evil. Any duplicity or dualism in our spirituality becomes clear to us in the illuminative stage. We begin to see things that we have struggled to deny in ourselves over the years. Courage is integral to the illuminative experience.

We have all learned from childhood how to do what family, school, social groups, and religious-formation processes expected of us. We learned implicitly and explicitly to put forth our best efforts for others. "Too good to be true" can characterize this self! It takes much longer to let go of the false self of self-preservation, or of other people's expectations, and become "too true to be good!" In finding acceptance as adults in our social world we have each paid a price. We have learned to compromise in some areas and not to do so in others. The faith dimension can also be dualist in experience—we can be caught between our desire to love authentically, and the price we have already paid to win the approval of others. This is the painful self-knowledge that typifies the illuminative experience. This is where we are exposed to the constrictions of our lives and faced with the possibility of freedom—which can be very frightening. We learn about our own darkness, areas where we lack freedom, our fears, and our shame. We want to say yes to our God, but there are new "enlightenments" of the extent of our own limits and of the power of God's love for us. We can be caught in the paralysis between the fear of receiving God's transforming love and the fear of what such love might mean in our ordinary relationships and commitments.

The illuminative way moves us away from the constraints of being conventional "nice people," and toward becoming more authentic selves-in-relationship. Greater self-awareness brings with it the freedom from attachment to our comfortable though constricted self-image or to the controlling opinions and expectations of others. Courage is essential for this development. Gradually we become aware that the evil and violence that we read about or see on our television screens are not just "out there." We recognize that we also have hatred, and anger and violence within ourselves. Good and evil are no longer issues apart from us. We experience our connectedness to the human race in a much more inclusive way than ever before. Through the movement of the Holy Spirit we experience illumination at our innermost depths of understanding, memory, and imagination. Patterns of personal and communal unforgiveness, of judgmental attitudes, of prejudice and exclusion come to light. In the illuminative way there is also a devastating awareness of our own emptiness before God. But, I, too,"if I persevere and pass through the angry darkness will discover in myself not only the evil and suffering of the world—at a deeper level I will discover the grandeur and beauty of God."[30]

A deep longing and sadness may also accompany this stage of our journey. The real issue that confronts us is how to take the appropriate steps to let the awareness of the living flame of God's love take shape within us: What do we embrace and accept within ourselves? What do we work to let go of? Part of the suffering of this stage comes from the emergent realization that incompleteness is part of the human condition. New levels of patience and trust are opened up to us. As we grow in understanding of our own capacity for evil and our fear of inner freedom, we grow in compassion for ourselves as well as for others. From personal acceptance of inner healing can come a healing of our relationships. Our actions can have communal consequences for good. "As the candle burns and gives light, so the mystic burns with the fire of love and radiates the light of wisdom."[31] Having befriended our limitations, we are enabled to reach out with a new openness to others in their struggle for authenticity. Our connectedness to others has new past, present, and future implications. Individualistic aspects of our life are subject to greater scrutiny than ever before in the illuminative way.

There is a temptation in the illuminative experience of raw openness to truth for people to try to be heroic or severe on themselves as a type of atonement or compensation for failure. Extra hours of prayer or harsh personal penances may be sought as an escape from the experience of being sinful or helpless before God. Such efforts are an attempt to escape the realization that we are unable to be "God" to ourselves. The experience of willed surrender to God in trust may be followed by times of closeness to God, along with a deep-down sense of peace, even in the experience of absence. Practices that have given us support in the past have now become hindrances, and the God with whom we have grown familiar is very much in the background—a one-dimensional being, dry and abstract. We find it hard to believe in God's love, knowing that our mistakes have been betrayals of that very love.

In our church communities as well as in society we are surrounded by experiences of conditional love and forgiveness. Our ideal self-image makes it harder for us to forgive ourselves when we do not live up to our own expectations. We can move into denial or projection to escape the pain of our failures. We may project the cause of our reaction onto others. We claim that their provocative behavior instigated the response that we find hard to deal with. So instead of putting the spotlight onto our inner world, we put it on the motivations of others. The illuminative way shows up escapist reactions we have chosen in the past and provides us with the opportunity to deal more authentically with these in the present.

John of the Cross maintains that the more we become disillusioned with our world and with our significant relationships the more we are drawn to desire God. We feel distaste for the things of God, and for everything else, along with a sense of profound aloneness. This experience of negation paradoxically indicates that a deeper communication of faithful loving has taken place within, but we only gradually tune in to its wavelength in our inner being.

We desire to turn to God in prayer, but we never seem to find what we are searching for. We find reasons for evading the solitude we yearn after, and at the same time we lament our evasions. The time of struggle in darkness brings us to greater inner-directedness, a greater adult interdependence with God as we get "tastes" of God, subtly and tantalizingly, but never to satisfaction. But if we give ourselves the time, we discover that in our bedrock depths within there is a dryness that is a quietness, a gentle aching awareness of God that is not concrete or tangible, not able to be cognitively accessed. There is a sense that this winter darkness is life-giving. Because God's gifts are being transferred from the world of our senses to the depths of our spirit, the darkness that ensues leads us to an inner-directed-ness, to self-acceptance, and to a new and de-centered experience. John of the Cross teaches that the purpose of spiritual darkness is to teach us to leave our ego behind in loving, so that we become capable of loving with God's own love. This radical turn about in loving has to be experienced in order to be understood.

This bedrock conviction of love, faith, and trust that we are moving to is graced. After these hard spiritual passages of confronting our false self and inner darkness, we know we have not earned what we have received. God wants to give us an abundance of love, and our dark-night experiences free us from the idea that we have to make God love us or that we have to work hard to receive God's love. By passing through the illuminative way we learn to accept that we are unconditionally loved by God, and that it is God's love that energizes us. This is a profound conviction that replaces all our earlier affirmations of faith and trust. We do not understand the "how" of this new understanding, but we do know that it is pure gift of God.

The Unitive Way: Graced Engagement with Love

After the de-centering experience of both the purgative and illuminative ways, there is a recentering in Christ, in one's God, that is described as transforming union. We have been through the crucible of freeing ourselves from the false self. "A non-possessive attitude toward everything, including ourselves, is established because there is no longer a self-centered 'I' to possess anything."[32] Our level of self-knowledge is more expansive and penetrating than before, and it has its foundation in our desire for and experience of God's transforming love.

> The desire for ever-deepening union with the Triune God, enkindled in the illuminative way, and the existential realization of one's absolute poverty and helplessness in the

125

face of the consuming desire for God's presence constitute
the threshold of transforming union.[33]

The fruit of this is a greater compassion toward oneself and others. As
a consequence, we are able to make a greater and deeper commitment
to service of others, because self-love is no longer at the center of our
motivations. We are ready to engage in undertakings that would have
daunted us in earlier stages. Our horizon of beliefs and values has
been transformed by this experience, and while we are able to plan
ahead, we live on a day-by-day continuum of trust.

Can we, in our ministry, assume that transforming union has not
been experienced by any of the people with and for whom we have
worked or ministered? Is this simply a theoretical experience that we
need only read about because we would never expect such experience
for ourselves or others? To believe this is to fail to realize that God's
self-communication in love is given according to God's will and God's
design, not according to our expectations. We would be unwise to
assume the absence rather than the presence of any experience of the
unitive way in our communities. This stage of Christian mysticism is
an indicator of fully authentic human living of eternal union with
God, which has its beginnings in this world.

This is a less self-conscious stance than those of earlier stages,
and there is a sense of both knowing and loving God through the
choices made and through the experiences of surrender that have
characterized past years of living and loving. Painful trust and peace-
ful waiting are counterpointed by experiences of sorrow and suffering. "Late have I loved you, beauty so old and yet so new; late have I
loved you....You touched me, and I am set on fire to attain the peace
which is yours."[34]

A new sense of personal aloneness is taking shape inside us, as
God's presence becomes more pervasive in our lives. We find ourselves less reliant on our senses, on satisfaction of our interests, and

even on our needs from time to time. We have a greater sense of communion with the human community.

> The mystic is experientially united to a love that communicates itself to all persons and to all things. Therefore, the more deeply the mystic experiences union with God, the more deeply union with God's creation is experienced. Transformed by and into Love itself, the mystic becomes creative, totally self-giving, radically concerned about others.[35]

There is more inner strength and energy to engage with life; whether we feel well or ill, we know we are engaging with the healing love of God for humankind and creation.[36] We may have physical or psychic pain, but at the same time there is a deep peace—often experienced as a dark, yet habitual awareness of God, a time of holy indwelling. It can be a time when, paradoxically, even in the experience of painful aloneness, deeper relationships are generated.

In the prayer of union, or infused contemplation,[37] God's transforming love reaches out to bring our imagination and memory into the process of integration and purification by which we are being re-created in Christ.[38] However, as we grow in inner healing and forgiveness, we may feel that we have regressed, because our memory may confront us with some "unfinished business" from our past. This remembering activity is often something utterly beyond our control or understanding. Yet it brings us face to face with healing of early memories that may have been too difficult to deal with at the time we experienced them. The healing of memories that is engaging us may be a healing of personal or familial memories. The process is a painful one—it costs—and its fruit is further self-discovery that is both painful and affirming. As memories come to the surface we are able to rework and integrate some of these memories into new understandings of ourselves and of our adult behavior patterns. We are

127

experiencing personal transformation as we heal our own memories and those handed on to us by our familial and societal heritage.

We may be sitting, walking, praying, or doing ordinary household things when a memory of a person, a place, or a happening comes to our consciousness. Sometimes this is a positive experience, and we connect with the experience in ways that affirm us. We feel connected with our past, with parents, siblings, and significant others who have gifted us in our early life, and their gifts echo within our being. At other times we can feel quite disturbed and distressed by a memory of how we have failed others, or how they have failed us. Anger can be generated by such memories. Sometimes the experience can be quite frightening. We can be assailed by a rush of memories, of feelings, of images that are disturbing. Spiritual writers advise that the best thing to do in this case is simply to be still; we should not try to analyze these rushing images but simply allow them to pass through us. Again, these can be opportunities for further healing in our self-understanding and in our ways of reviewing our difficulties in relationships. Sometimes we may bring them to our prayer or to spiritual direction. Some recurring memories may need the specific help of a counselor or therapist. The important issue at stake is that the difficult memory is an indication of potential for healing and development rather than of what has gone wrong with us. Times of healing of memories are times when, even in the experience of our painful aloneness, our relationships can be deepened by our growth in self-understanding and compassion. If, as ministers and religious educators we are able to give the time to attend to our own difficult and painful memories, an important aspect of middle adult spiritual development, then we will be better able to tune in to the opportunities for addressing the healing of memories in those we work with and for.

As we honestly accept some of the hard truths about our negative or destructive past choices or experiences, we realize that although we cannot change the facts of our past, we can change the way we understand them, and their consequences for our lives.[39]

128

Perhaps for the first time we learn what it is to accept God's forgiving love, not because we deserve it, but because God loves and forgives us because God is love! God's acceptance of us is far greater than our capacity to grasp this reality.

Self-knowledge, freedom, and compassion are major fruits of the unitive way. Self-knowledge, so much desired and yet feared, is one of the gifts of darkness that brings greater integration in life. With this new self-understanding comes a level of personal surrender that is experienced as a willing "letting go" of our controlling executive-self. This enables a mutuality and intimacy with one's God and one's closest friends that can only be dreamed of in earlier stages. When we have moved along the self-knowledge continuum, we find freedom. Freedom breaks through the boundaries from our past, both those we erected ourselves and those that others have imposed on us. We move into a time of new possibilities—no matter what our age, health, or activities may be.[40] Compassion, the ability to empathize with others, brings a readiness to reach out to others in their suffering. Again, in the heightened self-awareness of the unitive way, those areas of inner darkness that still need to be healed will be brought to the surface of our lives to be integrated in whatever way is appropriate. The courage to live compassionately comes from our acceptance of the mystery of the life, death, and resurrection of Christ, which finds an echo in our own suffering.[41] Compassion does not come from a self-absorbed withdrawal from the world; rather, the unitive way generates an active mysticism that connects us in solidarity with all people.

> Active mystics who live in the hurly-burly enter into the same inner silence as those who live in the desert. They experience the inner fire and the inner light; they experience the living flame of love that makes their being to be being-in-love. Now the inner fire drives them...to the crowded market place and to the inner city...to walk in peace marches, to demonstrate in the streets, to denounce

oppressive structures....Like the mystic in the desert they pass through agonizing dark nights and come to profound enlightenment.[42]

This "profound enlightenment" does not preclude further effort. More work may still need to be done with our neurotic weaknesses. These will continue to come to the surface to be dealt with.[43] Some of us with self-torturing temperaments will still have a struggle, but our temperament need not deprive us of the opportunity to heal the areas that impede our capacity for greater freedom in living and loving.[44]

It is not easy for us, with our Western heritage of Christian thought and our contemporary world of technological and scientific empiricism, to read what the mystics have described and to be able to use their wisdom to help us to interpret our own experiences, our own search for greater authenticity in our living and loving, in our own spiritual quest. Although spiritual writers speak about the three ways of the mystical journey as progressive stages to transforming union with God, there is a greater interplay among these ways than we might imagine. Rather than try to discover whether we are in one or the other of the three ways, we need simply to do our best to be authentic in our loving relationships with God, others, and God's world. We do not have to try to ascend the mystical ladder of transforming union. We can trust God to guide us.

We continue, throughout our lives, wherever we are in our mystical journey of living and loving, to discover things about ourselves, our family, and our society that it would be easier not to know. But in the knowing comes a new understanding, and in the understanding comes forgiveness, and from forgiveness flows compassion—the expansive God-given love—that reaches beyond the boundaries of our own pain and self-interest to others. Surely this is where the growth area of adult faith will be in the next decade or so, as people grow more attuned to the contemplative call to their inner world—a call not generated by their own needs but by the sheer gift of an unconditionally loving God.

Notes

1. Thomas H. Groome, "Total Catechesis/Religious Education: A Vision for Now and Always," in this collection of essays.
2. Colleen Griffith, "Spirituality and Religious Education: Fostering a Closer Connection," in this collection of essays. Griffith points out the dangers of the contemporary separation of spirituality and religion. Surely such a split has arisen from the nexus between religion and religious institutions. This problematic connection was explored in *The Mystical Element of Religion,* in which the purpose of a religious institution is presented as "to mediate, or communicate, the experience of the sacred, of God" (Baron von Hugel, *The Mystical Element of Religion* [New York: Crossroad, 1999; reprint of 2d ed., 1923], xiv).
3. Sandra Schneiders, "Feminist Spirituality," in *The New Dictionary of Catholic Spirituality,* ed. Michael Downey (Collegeville, Minn.: The Liturgical Press, 1993), 395.
4. Ann Carr, *Transforming Grace: Christian Tradition and Women's Experience* (San Francisco: Harper & Row, 1988), 203. Colleen Griffith's description of "education for 'wide-awakeness' with respect to the activity of God in people's lives" opens readers to lifelong implications of such an education for "spiritual maturity."
5. Tom Beaudoin, "Virtual Catechesis: Religious Formation of the Post-Vatican Generation," in this collection of essays.
6. Lifton studied the survivors of Hiroshima and described "psychic numbing" as a consequence of people's reaction to the realization that human beings are capable of destroying the earth. He explores what it means to live in the context of "mutually assured destruction" defense strategies. We repress the implications of the directions that our world seems to be taking. The despair, withdrawal, bouts of sadness and depressed feelings that are generated by our awareness of the potential for destruction that looms on the global horizon can be responded to either with the realization that we can do something to work toward the healing of humankind or with the psychic numbness Lifton describes—a numbness that leads us into a trivializing of our lives. This can also take place in regard to our spiritual lives. Consumerism and materialism can cause people to see God as a commodity. Spiritual overload and religious

numbing can also be generated by all the trappings of New Age spiritualities. Religious experience is consequently trivialized by such consumerist approaches. See Robert J. Lifton, *The Future of Immortality and Other Essays for a Nuclear Age* (New York: Basic Books, 1987). The terrorist bombings in New York City and in Bali may have also generated such a spiritual and psychic numbing response in viewers and listeners of media representations of the horror.

7. In the past the term *spiritual theology* usually encompassed asceticism and mystical theology. For a further clarification, see Kenneth Russell, "Ascetical Theology," in Downey, *The New Dictionary of Catholic Spirituality*, 63. For a more comprehensive approach, see Bernard McGinn, *The Presence of God: A History of Western Mysticism*, 4 vols. (New York: Crossroad, 1992–) The appendix to volume 1, *Theoretical Foundations: The Modern Study of Mysticism*, examines the authorities on the subject since 1900. I am grateful to William M. Johnston for this reference and for other suggestions.

8. James Wiseman distinguishes between two twentieth-century approaches to mysticism through their divergent understandings of the mysticism of Thérèse of Lisieux (James Wiseman, "Mysticism," in Downey, *The New Dictionary of Catholic Spirituality*, 682).

9. David Steindl Rast, *Gratefulness the Heart of Prayer* (New York: Paulist Press, 1984), 86.

10. Rahner points out that "mysticism is not confined to a privileged few....Mysticism cannot be reproached for being aloof from or hostile to the world....[It] is the truly dynamic element in the Church" (Karl Rahner, "Mysticism," *Sacramentum Mundi: An Encyclopedia of Theology* [New York: Herder & Herder, 1969], 4:138).

11. Harvey Egan, *An Anthology of Christian Mysticism* (Collegeville, Minn.: The Liturgical Press, 1991), xxii. Egan affirms Rahner's notion of the "mysticism of everyday life" but expresses an important concern about the possibility of equating Christian "piety, spirituality and mysticism" (xxiii). From an *interreligious* perspective, William Johnston describes mysticism as "the wisdom that goes beyond words and letters, beyond reasoning and thinking, beyond imagining and fantasy, beyond, before and after into the timeless reality. There are flashes of mysticism in the life of anyone who prays....But some people reach *a state of mysticism;* that is to say, they reach a state where this formless wisdom is always in their consciousness. This is the mystical state" (William Johnston, *"Arise My Love...": Mysticism for a New Era* [Maryknoll, N.Y.: Orbis Books, 2000], xvi).

12. Harvey Egan, *An Anthology of Christian Mysticism*, 600.

13. Herbert Benson, *Timeless Healing: The Power and Biology of Belief* (New York: Scribner, 1996), 196.
14. See Groome's essay in this collection.
15. Carolyn Bynum Walker points out the variations in the understanding of mysticism and spirituality: "Spirituality...was coined in the nineteenth century to designate a field of study that might also be called ascetic or mystical theology....Books on the history of medieval spirituality were surveys of various theories of the stages of the soul's ascent to contemplation or union." Bynum comments further that "the history of spirituality has come to mean something quite different: the study of how basic religious attitudes and values are conditioned by the society within which they occur...almost a branch of social history...dominated by an interest in popular religion" (Carolyn Walker Bynum, *Jesus as Mother: Studies in the Spirituality of the High Middle Ages* [Berkeley and Los Angeles: University of California Press, 1982], 3).
16. Bynum points out that "affective spirituality" of religious orders has been the dominant emphasis in much religious writing (Bynum, *Jesus as Mother*, 4).
17. William Johnston, *Mystical Theology: The Science of Love* (London: Harper Collins, 1995), 255; see also 256, n.43.
18. William Johnston, *Being in Love: The Practice of Christian Prayer* (San Francisco: Harper & Row, 1989). The mystical journey is of vital interest to Johnston and his key text that both maps and develops the theological foundation for mysticism is *Mystical Theology*.
19. Egan, *An Anthology of Christian Mysticism*, xvi.
20. Mystical writers such as John of the Cross use the metaphor of a spiritual ascent, even sketching the mountain climb, (see "The Ascent of Mount Carmel," in *Collected Works of St. John of the Cross*, rev. ed., trans. Kieran Kavanaugh and Otilio Rodriguez (Washington, D.C.: ICS Publications, 1991), 110–11. However, it may be useful to see the experience of the three ways, purgative, illuminative, and unitive, as recurring, more in terms of a growth spiral than a ladder.
21. This is also described as "the way of beginners." For a fuller theological approach to the *Via Purgativa*, see Johnston, *Mystical Theology*, 192–210.
22. Rowan Williams, *A Ray of Darkness* (Cambridge, Mass.: Cowley Publications, 1995), 101.
23. See Griffith's essay in this collection.
24. John of the Cross writes of the dark night of the senses and the dark night of the soul, "two different nights through which spiritual persons pass in both the lower and higher parts of their nature" ("The Ascent of Mount Carmel," 118).

25. The poles of postmodern attitudes described by Horell in his essay in this collection will surely resonate within today's faith-educating community. Tectonic changes have taken place in the catechetical world. Debates on naming the activity, philosophical and methodological issues, along with roles and membership within the educating community have engendered a wide range of reactions and responses, which are echoed in the larger society. Horell has encompassed them all. The personal and communal questioning that permeates our contemporary culture generates a questing faith that is as open to God's dynamic pedagogy as it is to established mainstream commitments and convictions.

26. Thomas Keating describes the false self as "the self developed in our own likeness rather than in the likeness of God; the self-image developed to cope with the emotional traumas of early childhood. It seeks happiness in satisfying the instinctual needs of security / survival, affection / esteem, and power / control, and bases its self-worth on cultural or group identification" (*Invitation to Love* [New York: Continuum, 1995], 145–46).

27. See Horell's essay in this collection.

28. Williams, *A Ray of Darkness*. Williams quotes John Donne: "He brought light out of darkness / Not out of a lesser light. / He can bring summer out of winter / Though thou have no spring" (104).

29. In his essay in this collection Horell notes that our postmodern culture "provides us with a chance to be more open, honest, and candid about ourselves and the world than we could be in the past." He reminds us that what we are experiencing personally in our educating and ministry resonates in the larger cultural context.

30. William Johnston, *The Mirror Mind: Spirituality and Transformation* (San Francisco, Harper & Row, 1981), 174.

31. Johnston, *"Arise My Love...,"* 119.

32. Keating, *Invitation to Love*, 103.

33. Thomas McGonigle, "Illumination, the Illuminative Way," in Downey, *The New Dictionary of Catholic Spirituality*, 987.

34. Saint Augustine, *Confessions*, trans. H. Chadwick (Oxford: Oxford University Press, 1991), X. xxvii (38), 201.

35. Egan, *An Anthology of Christian Mysticism*, xix.

36. The connectedness that is integral to the unitive stage is necessary in an era when, as Horell points out in his essay in this collection, "postmodern fragmentation profoundly affects the life of the church" as well as that of society itself.

37. Infused contemplation is pure gift of God, while contemplative prayer usually describes the efforts we make to rest contemplatively before our God, in contrast to the more usual discursive practice of meditation.

38. McGonigle, "Illumination, the Illuminative Way," 530.

39. One of the clearest expositions of such self-understanding can be read in Parker Palmer, *Let Your Life Speak* (San Francisco: Jossey Bass, 2000).

40. I am indebted to Joann Wolski Conn, *Spirituality and Personal Maturity* (New York: Paulist Press, 1989), for her helpful chapter about personal development and the dark-night experience.

41. Johnston points out: "It was precisely because he enjoyed the vision of the thrice-holy God together with the dire force of evil and darkness that Jesus suffered in Gethsemane. And the vision of God, far from making Jesus less human made him the most human of humans. Yet only the mystics understand Gethsemane. Only the mystics understand the dark contemplation that brings no joy or comfort (Johnston, *"Arise My Love...,"* 190).

42. Johnston, *Mystical Theology*, 364.

43. Joann Wolski Conn has presented the dark-night experience and implications of both darkness and nonclinical depression in *Spirituality and Personal Maturity*.

44. One woman who has undertaken the task of writing at some depth about the contemporary experience of living the unitive way is Bernadette Roberts (see *The Experience of No-Self: A Contemplative Journey* [Albany, N.Y.: State University of New York Press, 1993]). A former student, Barbara Bregler, introduced me to this author.